THE OCEAN OF MIRTH

The Ocean of Mirth brings together an English translation and an analytical interpretation of a singularly crucial, but obscure, Sanskrit medieval text, the *Hāsyārṇava-Prahasanaṁ* of Jagadēśvara Bhaṭṭāchārya. As a political satire, the volume finds significant resonances among contemporary questions of politics and society across the world, and examines the tension inherent in the clash of ideas such as freedom and order. In an unabashed celebration of disorder as the only way to fight violence, tyranny and autocratic impulses, *Hāsyārṇava* suggests no return to a Golden Age or to the rule of an iconic king; nor is there a promise of a saviour—a political farce that ends without any denouement in sight. One of the first authentic English translations of a neglected Sanskrit text from medieval India, this translation throws up interesting questions regarding values such as freedom, violence, order, chaos and disorder.

This volume will be a major intervention in the discovery of a significant non-canonical text of classical literature and will be indispensable for students, scholars and researchers of politics, philosophy, sociology, Indian literatures, Indology, comparative literature and culture studies.

Jyotirmaya Sharma is Professor of Political Science at the University of Hyderabad, India. In 2015–16, he was Visiting Fellow at the Institute for Human Sciences, Vienna. Between January and June 2012 he was a Fellow at the Swedish Collegium for Advanced Study, and Fellow of the Lichtenberg-Kolleg at the Georg-August-Universität in Göttingen, Germany, in 2012–13. He was also a member of the Scientific Advisory Council of the French Network of Institutes for Advanced Study, RFIEA, between 2013 and 2016. He is on the Scientific Advisory Board of Lichtenberg-Kolleg, the Göttingen Institute for Advanced Study, Germany. His recent publications include *A Restatement of Religion: Swami Vivekananda and the Making of Hindu Nationalism* (2013), *Cosmic Love and Human Apathy: Swami Vivekananda and the Restatement of Religion* (2013), *Hindutva: Exploring the Idea of Hindu Nationalism* (2015), *Terrifying Vision: M.S. Golwalkar, the RSS and India* (2007) and an edited volume titled *Grounding Morality: Freedom, Knowledge and the Plurality of Cultures* (co-edited with A. Raghuramaraju, Routledge, 2010).

THE OCEAN OF MIRTH

Reading *Hāsyārṇava-Prahasanaṁ* of Jagadēśvara Bhaṭṭāchārya, A Political Satire for All Times

Translated with an Introduction by Jyotirmaya Sharma

Routledge
Taylor & Francis Group
LONDON AND NEW YORK

First published 2020
by Routledge
2 Park Square, Milton Park, Abingdon, Oxon OX14 4RN

and by Routledge
52 Vanderbilt Avenue, New York, NY 10017

Routledge is an imprint of the Taylor & Francis Group, an informa business

British Library Cataloguing-in-Publication Data
A catalogue record for this book is available from the British Library

Library of Congress Cataloging-in-Publication Data
A catalog record has been requested for this book

ISBN: 978-0-367-27682-9 (hbk)
ISBN: 978-0-367-27827-4 (pbk)
ISBN: 978-0-429-29812-7 (ebk)

Typeset in Bembo
by codeMantra

MIX
Paper from responsible sources
FSC www.fsc.org FSC® C013056

Printed and bound in Great Britain by
TJ International Ltd, Padstow, Cornwall

For Martin van Gelderen and Antoinette Saxer

CONTENTS

Foreword: imagination and the returns of political freedom *viii*
Aishwary Kumar
Acknowledgements *xii*

1 Introduction 1

2 A note on the text and the translation 23

3 Name of characters in *Hāsyārṇava* in order of appearance 27

4 English translation of *Hāsyārṇava-Prahasanaṁ* 28

5 हास्यार्णवप्रहसनम् 60

References 79

FOREWORD

Imagination and the returns of political freedom

Freedom continues to pose one of the most intractable problems in Indian political thought. So problematic has been its philosophical and philological itinerary in Indian languages that political thought in India, insofar as it exists at all, has deemed it proper to leave its complexity nearly untouched. Indian Marxism has often, if not always, found in it little more than an inflection—or worse, subterfuge—of bourgeois value. Indian liberalism, on the other hand, unable to ever decisively break from the juridical traditions of classical vintage, has seen freedom merely as a civic extension—or as an instrument to re-entrench notions—of public morality. From that genealogy of morality, liberalism might still rescue a certain form of autonomy, a deep subservience to the moral law or *dharma*. Yet, as B. R. Ambedkar put it prophetically (and more than once, unapologetically), this autonomy would be anything but freedom. It is not surprising that the early translations of the idea of national self-determination spoke of freedom as *swadheenta*, which is, at best, when rendered back, 'autonomy' if not constraints—or even subordinations—of the self on (the imaginations of) the self itself.

Uses of vernacular substitutes for freedom abound, of course. Yet, among the many words that come close to 'freedom' in classical Indian traditions, *mukti* remains inadequately political because of its theological valence. *Swatantra* is mired in the liturgical apparatus, or, simply, the system (*tantra*) of sovereign power. And *swaraj*, by its very name, decidedly embroiled in the epistemic hubris and sacrificial militarism—*purusha*—that underpin the more mundane dimensions of the transcendent self or *atman*. The more glamorous—if barely more accurate—recent return of the self in Gandhian strands of Indian political thought as *swa* fails even more squarely to resolve the deepest impasse in Indian classicism: its tendency to succumb to the temptations of militarised mastery, of which Gandhi himself remains one of the most ambiguous exponents. Powerfully symptomatic of this epistemic militarism are the Brahmanic traditions of classical India, whose debilitating effects for democratic life, while seemingly archaic, have remained in our time anything but ancient.

What happens to 'freedom', then, in traditions that have never had a proper name or word for it? And if inaccurate, inadequate, perhaps even inappropriate translations of such a constitutively human idea were to be grafted onto such traditions—traditions that receive freedom as such with absolute silence (or deafening skepticism)—what would keep freedom from lapsing into visions of mastery, of sovereignty, of violence itself? Thinkers from traditions as diverse—even incommensurable—as Hannah Arendt and B. R. Ambedkar, Judith Shklar and Frantz Fanon, and more recently, David Shulman, Sumit Sarkar, Alf Hiltebeitel and Ranajit Guha have conducted at times scrupulous, at times sweeping and yet invariably painstaking archaeologies of this vanishing line between freedom and sovereignty.

In this tour de force of exegetical rigour and astute theoretical vision, Jyotirmaya Sharma joins the ranks of this distinctive constellation of thinkers, offering for the first time in Indian political thought—and for political theory as such—the most brilliantly counter-intuitive opening for such an archaeology of political freedom. Sharma's deceptively lucid but analytically rigorous anchor: 'satire' of seemingly classical, even archaic variety, albeit with implications more profound today than ever before, not least because of the relentless war on humour and dissent being waged by democratically elected governments worldwide. Readers of this groundbreaking work of interpretation will not fail to immediately notice something singular to Sharma's account of India's deep problems with freedom: his morally sustained, politically provocative and epistemologically just interest in the genealogies of political Hinduism—and religious violence as such—in modern India, to which he has already devoted a trilogy of transformative studies. Sharma brings to bear on his commentary on *Hāsyārṇava-Prahasanaṁ*, a seemingly premodern satire, his deep insight into the metamorphoses that religion has undergone in the Indian imagination under the stress of modern democratic yet rarely ever secular politics.

Seemingly premodern, one must qualify, simply because imagination becomes itself precisely by never leaving us. It leaves its context, its origins, its moment of birth behind, only to become a germ of a million beginnings. *Hāsyārṇava-Prahasanaṁ*, with all its sarcastic ambiguities and moral emergencies, gives Sharma a fecund ground to posit his most fundamental idea: the sheer, translucent and invisible ubiquity of (royal) power behind which it surreptitiously works and hides, creating at the same time a mesh of punitive principles, laws and obligations—let us, for the sake of simplicity, call this ironic mesh *nitidharma*—within which servitude and freedom thrive equally, in a sort of tragicomic equilibrium, as inverted images of each other. Not just in that distant past, which historicists love to call 'ancient India', but now, in the present: this present that is barely contemporary, this present that makes us struggle for breath that freedom requires, as if we were have never been modern. It is unsurprising that such a brilliantly lucid history of the present—pegged, with a Foucauldian finesse, on the stable head of one needle that is the *Hāsyārṇava-Prahasanaṁ*—is recovered not by a historian but a genealogist that Sharma is, one who sees in periodisation a ruse of sovereignty, in order a ruse of power, in disinterested classicism the ruse of intangible tyrannies.

Purists might take umbrage at such a world that Sharma asks us to return to (without ever renouncing the hermeneutic suspicion that modernity gives us). They might chaff at the suggestion that a world of such lucid inversions between freedom and servitude might be deemed moral at all, let alone political in the modern, democratic sense. Have the violent demands of *Shudradharma*, after all, not thrived precisely in this ambiguous mesh and spirit of the laws in which the Indian subject, never a citizen yet, finds domination—his and the other's—more tempting than liberty? Yet, is not that precisely Sharma's exact and exacting point: that Indian notions of freedom shall remain not so much as *inadequate* to modern political projects to be buttressed by puritan and purifying theories of Indian difference (a classic nationalist gesture now wholly typical of the urban Indian liberal) as they shall be fundamentally *inappropriate* to—even irreducibly inappropriable—by them?

This is where Sharma makes perhaps his most sensitive, supple and unconditionally just opening. If freedom is to be salvaged from civilisational visions of extreme nationalism, on the one hand, and vacuous universalities of neoliberal globalism on the other, it must be recovered not as a concept but as imagination; not in the grammatical language of the law but in the transgressive liberties of satire; not in the normative proprieties of courtly culture but at the ripping seams of inverted monarchism; not in the laws of genre but in the freedom of deviance. If the moral and political resources of such a freedom were to be sought in any sort of purist enterprise (humanist, nationalist, juridical or even idolatrously constitutional), freedom is bound to fail. In that sense, this is Sharma's *Hāsyārṇava-Prahasanaṁ*. For quite stunningly, his at once original and faithful commentary rescues the satire from Bhaṭṭāchārya's own hands, sounding a call not simply for a return to India's classical moral impasse—which I like to call, in the wake of Ambedkar, its *sovereign void*—but for a systematic, narrative reevaluation of the *place* of genre in it.

Whichever way one might look at it, Sharma's commentary, marked by his characteristic and copiously footnoted generosity towards scholars whose works he draws from and takes along on this timeless and inexhaustible quest of the political, is a work of sheer interpretive genius and methodological inventiveness. A commentary that brings out the extraordinary plasticity of meaning in Indian traditions—the elusive meaning of meaning (*arth*), one might add, without much exaggeration—rescuing the political from the tyranny of its normative certitude and its purportedly unproblematic translatability.

Of the clarity and purposefulness that Sharma displays as a translator, sensitively rendering not merely the technical meanings of words but attending to the theatrics of their breath and the drama of their tone, enough cannot be said.

What is important is that, in bringing alive the *theatre* that is satire, the theatre that is freedom, Hannah Arendt might say, with all its pauses and loquaciousness, Sharma recuperates not one text but an entire universe of jocular inversions and erotic transgressions, helping us find in those texts, treatises and techniques—all condensed in one word, *shastra*—our infinite power to reproduce and renew the work of freedom in something as mundane as a joke and as dissident as theatre. With a steady hand and deeply moral vision, Sharma transforms, in one sustained yet dazzling masterstroke, the tragic into the satirical and the humorous into something tainted ineradicably by the political. Could there indeed be a more fitting—and *inappropriable*—way to think the political today, with absolute freedom and equality?

Aishwary Kumar
Stanford University
March 2019

ACKNOWLEDGEMENTS

The inspiration to look seriously at *Hāsyārṇava* came with the invitation by Martin van Gelderen and Aishwary Kumar to a workshop on 'Freedom With and Without Europe: Indian and European Ways of Thinking', December 2017, Lichtenberg-Kolleg, Göttingen. I thank Martin van Gelderen, Aishwary Kumar, Shahzad Bashir, Serena Ferente, Humeira Iqtidar, Georgios Varouxakis and Vazira Zamindar for their comments.

To three individuals, I owe a deep and abiding sense of gratitude for bringing this book to life. As always, Sanjay Palshikar commented on several versions of the initial paper, and then on the introduction that accompanies this book. Rakesh Pandey first procured for me a copy of the Sanskrit version of the text and then became an intellectual collaborator every step of the way towards the making of this book—from the translation to the interpretation of the work. Kesavan Veluthat endorsed, encouraged and helped with the translation and with his deeply insightful comments on the introduction.

I also thank Sasheej Hegde and Akshara Ravishankar for their comments on the introduction. My gratitude to the two anonymous referees of the book whose invaluable observations made me improve the text. Pruthvi Sai M and Sahith M helped me prepare the final version of the text. My grateful thanks to Mr. KBV Krishna Mohan for preparing the Devanagari version of the original text.

Shashank S. Sinha at Routledge always believed in the book, made me believe in it more than I initially did and owned it in a way rare among editors and publishers today. It has been a privilege and a pleasure working with him, and I owe him a special debt of gratitude. Also, at Routledge, Aakash Chakrabarty and Brinda Sen have shown tremendous generosity, patience and commitment towards the book: I can't thank them enough. Grateful thanks are due to Jeanine Furino for seeing the production process through with unsurpassed professionalism.

This volume is dedicated to Martin van Gelderen and Antoinette Saxer. Over the years, they have offered me the gift of friendship in ways far too many to recount. Their friendship, to slightly paraphrase Montaigne, rules and sways with an absolute sovereignty.

1

INTRODUCTION

Hāsyārṇava, The Ocean of Mirth, is essentially a medieval Sanskrit political satire. At the centre of this complex and uncompromising text is a King. The King in *Hāsyārṇava* embodies chaos, the very opposite of what an ideal king must represent, namely, order. In a unique move, the text acknowledges and embraces the absence of order; there are moments in it that make the reader believe that behind the vast layers of satirical pronouncement, there is a fond, finely concealed wish to leave things in their messy and untended state. There might be subtle suggestions about the gifts that restoration of order might offer, bounties that order, when effectively enforced, often predictably brings. These gifts, sometimes real but more often imagined, also inevitably carry with them the real possibility of violence, cruelty, death and, above all, a curtailment and smothering of freedom. These untold bounties, then, are firmly and categorically spurned. Unlike almost all known political satires in India, this text offers no apologies for the chaos that lies at its heart.[1] In its unabashed celebration of disorder, *Hāsyārṇava* seeks no return to a Golden Age or to the rule of an iconic king. Neither does it announce the arrival of a wise sage or a learned brahmin to reinstate an ideal order. There is no promise of a saviour or an incarnation either. It is a political farce that ends without any denouement in sight. Consider this: all chaos, disorder, incompetence, weakness, decadence, sin, impropriety, indifference and, above all, the distortion of a sense of reality emanate from the King. It is equally true that these elements inhere in almost all the other characters as well; they are all an extension of the King.

The King's dramatic arrival is announced by the Naṭī, the principal female actor, just before the conclusion of the prologue in Act I. The Naṭī is preoccupied and absent-minded because the King is arriving to discuss matters of governance; voices from the wings inform that the King is coming to ascertain the welfare as well as misfortunes of the city's people. This is unusual because the King usually spends all his time in the women's quarter of his palace.[2] His arrival, then, could not be a good omen: to ward-off bad omen, it is recommended that empty, waterless pots be lined on the sides of the main street and lines be cast along the path of his arrival with needles of grain husk. The Sūtradhār, the principal male actor, clearly spells out his fears and apprehensions. Law, *nītī*, itself has been driven out of the kingdom to a far-off place and so have righteous men and women. Cheats, frauds and crafty people work relentlessly to defraud people of their wealth. Moreover, all men force themselves on the wives of other men to gratify their lust.[3] Having clearly spelt out the state of the kingdom, the Sūtradhār and the Naṭī leave to go elsewhere.

As the narrative progresses, we will discover that the King does not even make an appearance in Act II. But in Act I, the less than flattering initial picture painted by the Sūtradhār and the Naṭī considerably enhances as the political satire gets peopled by other characters. Bandhurā, Inclined-Vulva, the procuress, hails him as the 'universal monarch among the roguish' (*dhūrtānāṁ cakravartinaḥ*), and Kumativarmā, Protector-of-Folly, his minister, calls him 'the greatest sinner in the entire world', speaking openly of his meanness and his pitiable condition (*dainyaṁ*). The King is also fearful of sword-wielding thieves and feels unsafe in his palace. In a state of extreme disrepair and dereliction, the palace has no roof, snakes enter its precincts to feast on frogs, and the King and his Queen keep awake all night anticipating decayed walls to fall any moment.

If the King gives the impression of being weak and ineffective, he is not so in the full sense that Kauṭilya's *Arthaśāstra* describes:[4] he does not seem to be excessively violent and cruel in an overt sense. If murmurs of disaffection are heard among his subjects, the causes for their misfortunes are almost entirely traceable to the King and his actions. Despite the scare created in the prologue about his impending arrival, the King, throughout the narrative, emerges as a pathetic, indifferent and dissolute figure. After listening to an account of the state of the kingdom from the Servant-Spy, the King does promise to institute punishments (*daṇḍaṁ vidhāsyāmi*) for his subjects behaving badly, but that is the last time one hears the King express himself on the question of prescribing punishments. Though cases requiring dispensing of justice are brought to him, he rarely intervenes actively. His admits that his heart's innermost desire is to embrace a prostitute and gain access to an agreeable woman's lofty breasts, breasts that rise like an inaccessible mountain fortress.

On the contrary, insults are regularly heaped on the King. His minister, Protector-of-Folly, enters and greets him with his left hand. The royal preceptor, Viśvabhaṇḍa, World-Buffoon, enters Inclined-Vulva's house and ignores the King while greeting the procuress first. When the King greets World-Buffoon, the royal preceptor leaves the task of pronouncing a benediction for the King to his disciple, Kalahānkura, Tumour-of-Strife. In Act II, we will know that Tumour-of-Strife is only twelve years old. But in Act I, in offering blessings on

World-Buffoon's behalf, the depraved and vicious disciple begins by wishing that menstrual discharge appear from the King's eyes and continues:

> May your enemies grow, let your fears increase, may your ailments grow, let your debts and sins enlarge. May you attain the prosperity of misfortune and stupidity – may you attain these seven prosperities.
>
> *(Verse 21)*

Tumour-of-Strife's benediction is the closest we will come to a concise biography of the King. A portrait of misfortune, stupidity, debts, sins, ailments, fears and enemies is sketched with great precision and detail. These details are reiterated later by Mahāyātrika, Great-Beyond, the astrologer, but this time only by way of predicting the King's death. The King's 'final journey', reassures Great-Beyond, will help carry away the demon of his subject's misfortunes. In both instances, Tumour-of-Strife and Great-Beyond intone their 'blessings' and 'predictions' in the King's presence without any retaliation or recriminations.

All the flaws, limitations and sins of the King are steadily revealed by various characters throughout Act I. These flaws are in consonance with not being able to attain mastery over his senses as the *Arthaśāstra*[5] sternly recommends. Yet, setting aside momentarily the ideal expressed in the Dharmaṣāstras and the *Dharmasūtras*, nothing illustrates the King's condition better than his own name. He is King Anayasindhu. Two words join together to constitute his name. Sindhu is the sea or the ocean. In a geographical context, it could indicate the name of a river or the area around that river. An elephant, the water sprayed from the trunk of an elephant and the secretion coming out of the temples of an elephant are other ways in which the word could be understood. *Anayaḥ* carries the sense of bad management or conduct, injustice, unfairness, bad policy or course of conduct, evil course, but also conveys adversity, distress, misfortune, ill-luck and the propensity to gamble.[6] Given the various layers of meaning attached to *anayaḥ*, it is obvious that the King's character and actions find resonance with every single meaning of the word. Lee Siegel translates the King's name as 'Ocean-of-Misrule',[7] while David Shulman prefers to call him 'Ocean of Bad Policy'.[8] A close reading of the text, however, suggests that the King is a composite of all the shades of meaning attached to the word *anayaḥ*. Moreover, the word is being used for the King and not for an ordinary individual. Keeping this in mind, the name ought to be translated as Ocean-of-Disorder. Here are the reasons why King Anayasindhu is the Ocean-of-Disorder.

Let us recall that *nīti* has fled Ocean-of-Disorder's kingdom. *Nīti* refers to 'laws for kings', a much older set of technical instructions and rules of statecraft that constituted the early development of the idea of *rājadharma*.[9] We will return to the idea of *rājadharma* in the discussion that follows later in the chapter. But what is significant here is that the lack of attention to rules of statecraft on Ocean-of-Disorder's part has led to the collapse of *vyavahāra*,[10] indicating application of legal procedure and civil law. As mentioned above, a threat to prescribe punishments is brandished for a fleeting moment but not acted upon. The one instance in *Hāsyārṇava* where the King has an opportunity to dispense justice and apply the law is frittered away by the King's lack of attention due to various distractions in Inclined-Vulva's house and also by the remarkable incompetence of his minister. A bleeding resident of the city dragging Raktakallol, Joy-in-Blood, the barber, who has blinded him with a nail-clipping instrument, comes to the King for justice. The King explicitly asks Protector-of-Folly, his minister, to dispense justice to the resident of the city and the barber. After listening to both parties, Protector-of-Folly pronounces a judgement that amounts to grave injustice. During the entire process of hearing the case, and after the judgement has been given, Inclined-Vulva and Joy-in-Blood are heard sarcastically remarking that Protector-of-Folly is as 'eminent' as the King. This remark highlights a significant dimension in the narrative.

Kumativarmā, Protector-of-Folly, is the King's minister. He does the King's bidding unquestioningly. But he is unafraid of the King and calls him mean and the greatest sinner in the whole world. Only when the threat of armed thieves becomes imminent, he allows self-interest and self-preservation to triumph over his loyalty to the King: he wants to be protected even before the King and the Queen are secured. The King's magistrate Sādhuhiṁsaka, Tormentor-of-Righteous, is less concerned with sword-wielding thieves and more enthusiastic about meeting a prostitute. The army chief, Raṇajambuka, Jackal-of-War, manages to hollow out a bee with his sharp sword and faints and falls at the sight of anything resembling blood. In other words, the ineffective and dissolute nature of the King extends to all his officers and his ministers.

★

In pre-classical and classical India, the relationship between the kṣatriya king and the brahmin priest is endlessly rehearsed as an ideal. They both confine themselves to distinct spheres but also collaborate to wield power over the kingdom. Similarly, the brahmins as priests and the kṣatriya as warriors, representing hierarchically organised social castes and classes, together rule over everyone else in society. The reality might have been very different: after all, it is perfectly possible for physical and military power of the kṣatriya to overwhelm the 'weapons' of the brahmins, namely, ritual sacrifice and learning. A very mixed and often contradictory picture of collaboration, fear, loathing, distrust and serving mutual self-interest emerges from this relationship.[11] But in the interstices of the same tradition, there are equally countless examples of the inherent weakness of the king. Independent of the hyperbolic accounts of the king's power, autonomy and supremacy,[12] the king has very little space to infinitely manoeuvre and act as he may wish. At least the manner in which the ideal is unveiled, he is checked by the undisputed hierarchical superiority of the brahmins and their counsel.[13] Vaśiṣṭha, a late first-century B.C.E. authority on dharma, states the ideal unambiguously: 'The three social classes shall abide by the instructions of the Brahman. The Brahman shall proclaim the dharmas, and the King shall govern accordingly'.[14]

In order to understand the collapse of the brahmin-king relationship in *Hāsyārṇava*, let us recall the single most significant piece of advice that Kauṭilya's *Arthaśāstra* offers the king:

> Mastery over the senses consists of the senses – ear, skin, eye, tongue, and nose – not wandering inappropriately among sounds, touches, visible forms, tastes, and smells; or rather, putting into practice what the treatise prescribes. For this entire treatise boils down to the mastery of the senses. A king who behaves contrary to it and has no control over his senses will perish immediately, even though he may rule the four ends of the earth.[15]

If the argument that almost all characters in this political satire are an extension and elaboration of King Ocean-of-Disorder's personality and actions, then it seems that *Hāsyārṇava* boils down to a determined and impudent rejection of this precautionary advice Kauṭilya proffers. After all, the *Arthaśāstra* expects the king to curb his senses, and, in doing so, 'shun the wives and property of others and refrain from causing injury, as also from sloth, frivolity, falsehood, wearing lavish clothes, associating with pernicious individuals, and transactions that go against Law or Success'.[16]

A later text, *The Law Code of Manu*, aligns the idea of the king's success in subduing his senses to his ability to bring his subjects under control. In Manu, the list of vices also multiplies: ten vices arising out of pleasure, eight emerging from anger. Both these set of vices, in turn, find their beginnings in greed.[17] Both texts, however, distrust the king's ability to be disciplined on his own. The *Arthaśāstra* recommends that the king must appoint teachers or ministers to set limits, keep the king away from harmful situations and not let him indulge excessively in private pleasures and waste his time.[18] But most important among these appointments is that of the counsellor-chaplain. Once appointed, the king ought to follow the counsellor-chaplain as a student follows a teacher, the way a son follows his father and the manner in which a servant obeys his master.

> Royal power (kṣatra) set ablaze by the Brāhmaṇa, consecrated by mantras consisting of the counsel (mantra) of the counsellor (mantrin), and protected by the weapon (śastra) consisting of following the treatise (śāstra) conquers without being conquered.[19]

Manu suggests that the king consult an intelligent and distinguished priest about the most important elements of his sixfold policy, have confidence in him and entrust all his matters to the priest.[20] This is not to be confused with the king's need to appoint personal and officiating priests for domestic rituals and sacrificial rites.

Far from controlling and keeping a check on the King's actions, *Hāsyārṇava* has the most staggering confluence of corrupt and decadent brahmins if viewed from a *Dharmaṣāstra* perspective. It is unique in the sense that it offers no brahmin character who seems to uphold the brahmin ideal even in a diluted sense. The World-Buffoon is acknowledged by the King as his family priest, someone he calls a 'great preceptor'. But before his arrival, Inclined-Vulva tells us in a subtle use of the word 'upādhyāya' that he was not just a mere preceptor or a religious teacher but someone who gave instructions for wages and, hence, inferior to an 'āchārya'. Despite wearing ochre robes and holding an elegant staff, he eats food that is taboo, desires whoring and is the crest-jewel of the perfidious. As the political satire unfolds, we encounter brahmins, brahmin preceptors, brahmin priests, brahmin disciples and brahmin astrologers. All of them are crafty and wicked. Again, their names are illustrative of their character: World-Buffon, Tumour-of-Strife, Blind-with-Passion, Wild-Cock, Mighty-Censurer, Ocean-of-Deceit and Predictor-of-the-Great Beyond.[21]

Beyond their suggestive names and deviant characters, all the brahmins in the narrative either flout the conventional rules of their caste openly or express disdain for their traditional roles. In an unusual outburst, Tumour-of-Strife questions the value of serving his preceptor, ritually worshipping the sun, rigorously studying the Vedas and even the ultimate futility of attaining heaven. A fascinating character among the 'fallen' brahmins, Madanāndhamiśra, Blind-with-Passion, loves hemp liquor, gets his sacred thread smeared red from the unguents of prostitutes and, above all, has distaste for religious service. He rejects distressing practices such as fasts and other bodily mortifications and advocates propitiating Lord Shiva with meat, fish and women. World-Buffoon and Blind-with-Passion are not averse to quoting the epics to justify their unsavoury pursuits. Mahānindakācārya, Mighty-Censurer, considers himself to be the most erudite brahmin in the whole cosmos. Not confined to this bombast alone, he claims that he, and not Lord Brahmā, had composed the Vedas, thereby undermining the divine origins of these pre-eminent texts.

★

If we look at pre-classical, classical and medieval texts relating to the brahmin-kṣatriya relationship in general, and the king-counselor-chaplain dynamic in particular, differences in emphasis and in designating actual power abound.[22] There is one element, however, that transcends all textual contradictions and historical periodisation in relentlessly and consistently defining the ideal king and his royal functions. This is the desire and pursuit of order. One of the early texts describing a Vedic sacrifice vividly invokes the centrality of maintaining order.

> And as to why they mutually hand it on [the wooden sphya wielded in the sacrifice] in this way, they do so lest there should be a confusion of classes, and in order that [society or kingdom] may be in the proper order.[23]

In these early formulations, the king's duty is to safeguard the integrity of the four social classes (*varṇa*) and the four stages of life (*aśrama*). Vaśiṣṭha enjoins that 'the king should make the four classes adhere to the dharma proper to each'.[24] Kauṭilya is clear about maintaining this order because it is the *dharma* or law that the Triple or the three Vedas—Sāma, Ṛg and Yajus—had laid down:

> Therefore, the king should not permit people to violate the Law specific to each of them, for when they adhere to the law specific to each they rejoice here and in the hereafter.
>
> When among a people, the bounds of the Ārya way of life are firmly fixed and the social classes and orders of life are firmly established, and when they are protected by the Triple, they prosper and do not perish.[25]

Once he fully comprehends the mandate of preserving the *varṇāśrama*, the *Dharmasūtras* and the *Dharmaṣāstras* also expect him to protect all creatures and give them the guarantee of security and protection. Here are a few examples of what the *Dharmasūtras* say:

> To a king pertains, in addition, the protection of all creatures, as also meting out just punishment.
>
> *Gautama, 10.7–8.*[26]

> To take care of creatures is the special duty (dharma) of a king, and he attains success by fulfilling it... After enquiring into all the Laws specific to various regions, castes, and families, the king should make the four classes adhere to the Laws proper to them and punish them when they deviate from them.
>
> *Vaśiṣṭha, 19.1; 19.7–9.*[27]

Preserving the *varṇa* and the *aśrama* order, protecting people and punishing people deviating from order become the foremost duties of the king. His mission and function is a *dharma*, a form of duty. In the words of an authoritative text from the classical period, 'the law [dharma] is here the ruling power standing above the ruling power'.[28] *Dharma*, then, implies a way of behaving, a right way in which to behave and the way in which one should behave, that is, one's duty.[29]

In the evolution of the idea of the ideal king in *Dharmasūtra* and the *Dharmaṣāstra* literature, two broad strands can be seen. The first is the early emphasis on 'rules for the kings' comprising technical instructions in legal procedure. In this phase, most texts speak of the duties of the king, 'rājadharmas', in the plural.[30] In the second part of the theme, such duties and royal functions of the ideal king as keeping order, protecting people, handing out punishments are expanded, elaborated and subsumed under a distinct category called *rājadharma*. This is an omnibus notion that circumscribes all other constellations of a king's *dharma*. In an evocative phrase, Mark McClish calls it the 'syncretic concentration of all royal activities under *rājadharma*'.[31] By the time we reach the period of Manu's law codes, this second strain becomes pervasive and authoritative:

> A kṣatriya who has received the vedic consecration according to rule has the obligation to protect this whole world in accordance with the norms; for when people here are without a king and fleeing in all directions out of fear, to protect this whole world the Lord created the king by extracting eternal particles from Indra, Wind, Yama, Sun, Fire, Varuṇa, Moon, and the Lord of Wealth.
>
> Because the King was fashioned out of particles from these chiefs of the gods, he overpowers all beings by reason of his energy. Like the sun, indeed, he burns eyes and minds; no one on earth can bear the gaze upon him. He is Fire, he is Wind, he is the Sun, he is the Moon, he is the King of the Law [Yama], he is Kubera, he is Varuṇa, and he is the Great Indra – by reason of his power.[32]

Manu is clear that the world will be a fearful chaos without a king. The king must enforce the norm. Though the king is not himself divine, assisting him in this task of establishing order are his divine origins and his considerable power. In this later phase of development of *rājadharma*, many elements absent in earlier stages get attached to the ideal. The king's actions now have ethical implications for this world and for the purposes of attaining a better afterlife. The whole duty of the king attains the status of a religious activity that includes granting gifts and favours to brahmins, being mindful that the merits and sins of his subjects become part of his cumulative actions and, finally, perceiving his role in terms of a ritual sacrifice and a sacred vow.

★

Crucially, there is, however, a prerogative attached to the royal function that is unique to the king. This is *daṇḍa*, or punishment. Literally meaning, 'mace', 'rod' or 'sceptre', it is an institution that is created to look after the king's interests, enable him to establish order, enforce norms and protect his subjects. The earliest accounts of the role of the king attest to the significance of *daṇḍa*. The Āpastamba Dharmasũtra classifies punishment and warfare under the duties of a kṣtríya, while Gautama Dharmasũtra lists the king's role as protecting all creatures and meting out just punishment; in Vaśiṣṭha, the king is asked to punish those that deviate from the law prescribed for each of the social classes.[33] In the pages of Manu's law codes, *daṇḍa* comes to be personified as the Lord's son made from the energy of Brahman. Some of the most striking lines in the chapter titled 'The Law for the King' in *The Law Code of Manu* are reserved for describing *daṇḍa*, the son of the Lord:

> It is fear of him that makes all beings, both the mobile and the immobile, accede to being used[34] and not deviate from the Law proper to them...

> Punishment is the king; he is the male; he is the leader; he is the ruler; and, tradition tells us, he stands as the surety for the Law with respect to the four orders of life. Punishment disciplines all the subjects, Punishment alone protects them, and Punishment watches over them as they sleep – Punishment is the Law, the wise declare.[35]

Manu perceives the king to be the one who administers punishment. In doing so, he has to be truthful, wise and have mastery over the three *puruṣārthas*, namely, *dharma* or Law, *artha* or Wealth and *kāma* or Pleasure. Punishment, then, must be meted out judiciously, carefully and correctly. Failure to do so rebounds on the king by creating total havoc. Despite these disclaimers regarding the unwise use of punishment and the obsessive quest to establish *dharma* as duty and prevent deviations or *adharma*, these texts forge an extraordinary relationship between the ideal king and punishment.

The king is often called *daṇḍadhara*, meaning both the carrier of the sceptre and the upholder of punishment. There are texts that often use the words 'king' and 'punishment' synonymously and interchangeably.[36] Both sets of texts, the earlier ones like Vaśiṣṭha and Gautama, and later ones like Manu, also affirm that while inflicting punishment as part of his royal functions, the king remains untainted and no impurity attaches to him.[37] Citing Manu, Alf Hiltebeitel calls the facility of the king wielding *daṇḍa* being endowed with 'statutory purity' or 'instant purification', leaving him immune to the impurity of bloodshed.[38] In Madeleine Biardeau's memorable formulation, for the king, the 'violence inherent to royal *dharma* and to well-regulated exercise of *daṇḍa* poses no peculiar problem'.[39]

The phrase 'violence inherent to royal *dharma* and to well-regulated exercise of *daṇḍa'* mirrors the normative-textual tradition's incessant reiteration of the primacy of an immutable *rājadharma* aided by the fearsome *daṇḍanīti*. In the epic, the *Mahābhārata*, 4509 verses and 128 chapters are devoted to the discussion of *rājadharma* alone. Of these, Chapter 1343 is central to any understanding of punishment and its undisputed primacy. It also represents the most articulate expression of *rājadharma-daṇḍanīti* framework. Its setting is a monologue uttered by Arjuna, the warrior-prince, to Yudhiṣṭhira, the new king. Arjuna begins in dramatic fashion:

> The rod punishes all subjects. The rod protects them. When everything is asleep, the rod is awake. The learned say that the rod is dharma. O lord of men! The rod protects both dharma and artha. The rod protects kāma…In this world that has come about, everything is based on the rod…To ensure that there was no confusion among mortals, to protect riches and to establish boundaries in this world, daṇḍa was thought of. When daṇḍa strides around, dark and red-eyed, there is exultation and subjects are not confused.[40]

In the first few verses of the chapter, the operative words are 'fear' and 'frightened'. Soon these are substituted effortlessly with arguments that support, endorse and justify killing. Gods kill, Time kills, Death kills. Certain gods are worshipped because they have killed. Everyone alive in the world acts violently; the stronger live off the weaker. Only the stupid control their anger (and delight) and retire to the forest. If *daṇḍa* did not exist, the world would be destroyed. The rod controls the four social categories/castes, preserves boundaries, legitimises property, maintains the difference between the virtuous and the wicked and ensures the observance of the four stages of life. Righteous violence, represented by *daṇḍa*, sustains *dharma*, which, in turn, sustains the world.[41] Moreover, *dharma*, *artha* and *kāma* exist under the rod's protection, as indeed does everything in the world.

Dharma, then, cannot exist and prosper in disorder: in Manu's words, disorder leaves everything topsy-turvy. If disorder is seen as an imbalance among social classes, with limits being breached and insecurity growing among subjects, punishment has to step in and restore order. Borrowing certain striking phrases from the *Mahābhārata*, Manu elaborates:

> The whole world is subdued through Punishment, for an honest man is hard to find; clearly, it is the fear of Punishment that makes the whole creation accede to being used. Gods, demons, Gandharvas, fiends, birds, and snakes – even these accede to being used only when coerced by Punishment. All the social classes would become corrupted, all boundaries would be breached, and all the people would revolt as a result of blunders committed with respect to Punishment. Wherever Punishment, dark-hued and red-eyed, prowls about as the slayer of evil-doers, there the subjects do not go astray – so long as its administrator ascertains correctly.[42]

In other words, in a world falling apart, restoring order is possible only by violence integral to the *rājadharma-daṇḍanīti* framework.[43] It is a vicious cycle: the king desires order, and in ensuring this, he exceeds the proper limits of *dharma* by containing disorder through violence and by killing. This leaves him weak, contaminated with evil, vulnerable, confused, flawed, unbalanced, crippled and frustrated. Nothing could be more cruel than the *dharma*-law-duty order. '*[D]aṇḍa* stands at the intersection of the political and legal', writes McClish, 'the normalisation (in a literal sense) of domination, where coercive violence becomes just punishment'.[44]

In the passages from a variety of sources cited above, the question of the *puruṣārthas* recurs with great frequency. Manu expects the ideal king to have mastery over law, wealth and pleasure. In discussing *rājadharma*, Arjuna cites the learned to argue that *daṇḍa* is, indeed, *dharma* or law itself. He also says that *daṇḍa* protects *dharma*, *artha* and *kāma*. It has long been believed that the pairs of three or four *puruṣārthas* showcase the practical as well as theological concerns. This needs a brief explanation. The early *Dharmaśāstras* list only *dharma*, *artha* and *kāma*, whereas later texts add *mokṣa* or liberation to the list. Most commentators[45] acknowledge an essential tension in understanding the three *puruṣārthas*, the areas of disagreement coalescing around two questions. One is the primacy and superiority of *dharma* among the three, and the second is the seeming interdependence of the three. It is useful to recapitulate that Manu makes the three *puruṣārthas* dependent on the proper exercise of *rājadharma* led by a forceful *daṇḍanīti*.[46]

In another influential reading of the *puruṣārthas*, Charles Malamoud[47] suggests that the relative emphasis on any given set of *puruṣārthas* is driven by the context of the philosophical reflection. So, for instance, in Vedānta, the configuration could be 2+2, where *kāma* and *artha* indicate *preyas* or 'what is pleasant', and *dharma* and *mokṣa* point towards the *śreyas* or 'sovereign good'. Citing what he calls the 'revolving hierarchy of *puruṣārthas*', Malamoud suggests that privileging a particular *puruṣārtha* depends on the *varṇa* and *āśrama* of an individual as well as the determining of an ultimate aim in life. But because these activities undertaken by an individual, notwithstanding his *varṇa* or *āśrama*, fall within the ambit of his *svadharma*, it is safe to conclude that *dharma* encompasses all activities. Moreover, a single *puruṣārtha* might indicate a narrow and a wide meaning. Artha, for example, might mean wealth and material goods in the narrow sense but also imply 'motive' in the wider sense. This would transform all *puruṣārthas* to mean '*artha*' since they are motives for certain kinds of action. Similarly, *dharma* too, in the narrow sense, might mean following Vedic rituals and observances but might also mean, in the wider sense, the ways in which the *varṇas* and *āśramas* regulated and governed.

Donald Davis, Jr., has challenged this conventional understanding of the *puruṣārthas*.[48] For him, they are neither essential nor distinctive; indeed, he rejects the idea that they are values. If one stops privileging the '*artha*' or goal and aim part of the composite term, that is,, *puruṣārtha*, and let the stress fall on *puruṣa* or human or person, then we move away from a view that sees *puruṣārthas* as values that impel action; we, then, begin to perceive them as actions plainly, or principal categories and spheres of human activity. In most text, he argues, the *puruṣārthas* are nothing more than a theory of human needs and activities geared towards attaining the 'good life' in a purely worldly sense. Embracing the totality of human life, as concepts, they seem like sweeping abstractions. Hence, many texts move the focus of the *puruṣārthas* to explaining in great detail the whole gamut of activities undertaken within each *varṇa*. Calling their importance as rhetorical in nature, he asserts that the *puruṣārthas* act as a stereotyped frame for speaking about human pursuits.

★

If the synoptic view of the *Dharmasūtra* and the *Dharmaṣāstra* literature illuminates anything, it reveals how radically distant King Ocean-of-Disorder and all he represents are from the portrait of the ideal king and of *rājadharma*. We already know that the Naṭī announces the state of overall collapse even before the King's arrival. After he arrives, the King asks the Servant-Spy to ascertain the state of the kingdom. The King calls him an 'expounder of false perceptions' even before the Servant-Spy completes his assigned task. Soon, the 'expounder of false perceptions' returns and reports on the conduct of the King's subjects. He speaks with great concern about all the social classes and castes adhering to their designated roles; he attests to ethics and morals being in place and swears that women wear jewellery the way it must be worn. The Servant-Spy calls this state of affairs confusing and nonsensical and tells the King that his kingdom and his subjects exhibit an extreme transgression of rules. This exchange between the King and the Servant-Spy hides a very complex equation.

Even before he presents his report, the King knows that the Servant-Spy is prone to presenting false perceptions. On hearing the Servant-Spy's account, in ordinary circumstances, the King ought to have realised that the opposite of what the Servant-Spy is saying ought to be the truth. Predictably, true to his reputation, the Servant-Spy presents a distorted and untruthful picture of reality. And equally interestingly, the King believes the untrue and distorted version to be true. He even promises to rectify the state of affairs by instituting punishments (*daṇḍaṁ vidhāsyāmi*). If the Servant-Spy is an expounder of false perceptions, then the King is a believer in false perceptions. The Naṭī reveals the true state of the kingdom, the Servant-Spy gives a false version of reality, and the King believes the false version to be true. Is this a case of inversion of reality? Or is it, as Shulman suggests, an instance of a 'kind of order that disorder can represent'?[49]

A clue to these questions might lie in the text. When the barber called Joy-in-Blood enters the makeshift court of the King in Inclined-Vulva's house, he presents the King a mirror. The King refuses to even hold it and asks Inclined-Vulva to take it. Suffering from cataract, she has no use of the mirror, which is ultimately taken by the World-Buffoon. The King has no interest in reality; he knows that the mirror would reflect nothing but him in many roles and guises. He knows that looking into a mirror, he will see only his image, one that extends to everyone and permeates everything. After all, even at the outset, when the Servant-Spy gives him a distorted picture of reality, something significant doesn't strike him. The reality that is presented to the King is presented as a collapse of order and of legal procedure. Yet, what is presented is actually the *Dharmasūtra* and the *Dharmaṣāstra* ideal likened by the Servant-Spy as a confused and nonsensical state. He refuses to acknowledge the ideal, affirms that the elements of the ideal as presented to him constitute a transgression and, as a result, promises punishment.

Is disinterest on Ocean-of-Disorder's part in the compelling myth of the iconic king and in the *rājadharma-daṇḍanīti* framework such a fatal flaw?

It is no surprise that the King in *Hāsyārṇava* is called the Ocean-of-Disorder. Neither is it unusual that almost all other characters in the play are an extension of the disorder that the King so vividly personifies. This is disorder at its best: hierarchies weaken or collapse, insecurity thrives, the powerful torment the weak,[50] the weak retaliate when given a chance, boundaries disappear, wealth gets freed from the *dharma*-framework and so does erotic love, well-worn pieties dissolve, derisive laughter resounds, mediocrity triumphs, creativity finds release, fidelity to customs and traditions dissipates, rituals become meaningless, judgement flounders. It is this breach in the *dharma*-fortress that constitutes an instance of freedom. Recall again that the 'dark and red-eyed' *daṇḍa* protects *artha* and *kāma*.[51] Freedom is *artha* and *kāma* freed from the stranglehold of *dharma*.[52] *Artha* is not merely 'wealth', 'opulence', 'money', 'utility' or 'advantage'. It also means 'aim', 'purpose', 'cause', 'motive', 'reason', 'sense'. *Kāma*, too, is not erotic pleasure alone, but also 'desire', 'longing', 'love', 'affection'. Disorder enables *artha* and *kāma* to run berserk. Freedom, then, is this small, perhaps even short-lived, opening between order and chaos.

Hāsyārṇava implicates its characters in disorder with a degree of such generous plenitude that there is little possibility of a *dharma*-backlash. The King, his ministers and the brahmins are all estranged from the ideal to such an extent that the possibility of staving off any potential violence to restore order does not even arise. In this chaos, it is not so much that the big fish devour the small fish. Rather, Mithyārṇava or Ocean-of-Deceit, the brahmin, who comes to consult the court for ways of atonement after the lynching of a brahmin, correctly captures the driving force in *Hāsyārṇava*: it is leeches living on the body of leeches.

★

There is little doubt that *Hāsyārṇava* is a significant political satire. It represents disorder and chaos in a fundamental sense. But it is also significant that the entire narrative unfolds in the house of a prostitute; indeed, the King holds court in her house. Also, from the prologue onwards, there is a strong erotic element that persists throughout the two acts of the satire: its self-description itself is of a poem which is 'like a fair-complexioned woman, who is free, spontaneous, self-willed and capable of generating wild emotions'. While a lot of the erotic element in the text would be alien and distasteful to some contemporary sensibilities, there is a need to understand it for a number of reasons. There is little in the play that is prudish or inhibited. No character, man or woman, exhibits even a degree of discomfort with the bodies or their sexual needs, however misplaced these needs may seem to be. While there are several verses that starkly demonstrate lascivious men lusting after the bodies of women, in each instance, their lustful pronouncements reflect adversely on their character. Every attempt, verbal or actual, to embrace Streak-of-the-Young-Moon's-Crescent shows these men as flawed, inadequate, incomplete and pathetic.

Sexual excess and gluttony are marked in a sharp and distinct relief at the outset. The Prologue sets the tone. It illustrates the love-making of Śiva and Parvati. While the verses seem not too original, they remind us of passages from the 'Umāsuratvarṇanaḥ' or 'The Description of Umā's Pleasure', the eighth sarga of Kālidāsa's *Kumārasaṃbhavam*[53] but also the Pārvatīkhaṇḍa of the Rudreśvara Samhitā in the *Śiva-Purāṇa*.[54] A cursory look at verses 7 and 8 in *Hāsyārṇava*, verses that have a fulsome description of the spring and its erotic promise, would remind the reader of similar passages in Jayadeva's *Gītagovinda*, a celebration of the love between Krishna and Radha.[55] This divine amorous play manifests in the world in the form of spring, itself a metaphor for the erotic. No character in the play other than the women conforms to either the model of divine erotic love or the erotic promise of regeneration of the senses that the spring promises. They merely represent an insatiable, limitless appetite.

Let us take an example to illustrate some of the aforementioned points. In Verse 8, we are told that the Mādhavikā vines laden with flowers are embracing the mango tree with joy, but this embrace also may seem like 'instructing a newly-wed bride in the art of making love'. We also know that at least two brahmins have been commissioned by Inclined-Vulva to instruct Streak-of-the-Young-Moon's-Crescent in the art of making love. Nothing could be in greater contrast than the imagery of the embrace of the Mādhavikā vines and the prospect of being embraced by these two brahmins. World-Buffoon, the royal preceptor, is the first. He is the crest-jewel of frauds and despite his ascetic garb, his interests are focused entirely on whoring. Moreover, he is supposed to be a paid instructor. Following the *Kāma Sūtra*, it is unlikely that he is a paid instructor. Rather, he could be a steady lover. The *Kāma Sūtra* suggests that with a steady lover, the courtesan pretends to be his pupil, plays innocent and ignorant of erotic techniques while making love and asks him to teach her.[56] Blind-with-Passion is the second instructor. He too is a debauched brahmin who has given up all pretensions about leading a life of religious service. But like the rest of the men, he keenly anticipates sleeping with a prostitute. Streak-of-the-Young-Moon's-Crescent is self-willed and self-possessed and contemptuously mocks the old men lined up by her mother[57] to 'instruct' her.

What about the King's position in relation to the erotic? He too desires to embrace a prostitute: it is his heart's innermost desire. The only time he speaks of weapons and war is when he speaks of amorous battles. He likens his entry into Inclined-Vulva's house to having attained the merit of a hundred pilgrimages. In the *Arthaśāstra*, prostitutes are allowed in the royal residence after 'they have cleansed their bodies by bathing and rubbing and changed their clothes and jewelry'.[58] The *Arthaśāstra* ensures the appointment of a superintendent of courtesans,[59] designates that the residence of the prostitutes be located in the southern direction of the fort along with dancers and Vaiśyas,[60] enumerates the fee for sex with a prostitute[61] and prescribes penalties for sex with a prostitute by force as many men used to rape prostitutes.[62] While the *Arthaśāstra* accords a degree of respectability to prostitutes, they are placed in the bottom-half of the hierarchy of social classes and caste, not outside the ambit of the social classes. Though the *Arthaśāstra* is silent on the question of a king visiting the house of a prostitute, the *Kāma Sūtra* strategically curtails the amorous proclivities of the king, expressly prohibiting the king and his ministers from entering other people's houses on the grounds that such conduct of the powerful is bound to be emulated by the subjects.[63] Clearly, King Ocean-of-Disorder and his ministers violate every norm prescribed in the *Arthaśāstra* and the *Kāma Sūtra*.

Since disorder and transgressing boundaries is the primary purpose of *Hāsyārṇava*, none of this ought to surprise the reader. However, the presence of an unrestrained libido among all male characters and the violation of norms by the powerful do not adequately explain the rampant eroticism in the text. In reading another such satire, Donald Davis, Jr., has sought to explain[64] the surfeit of eroticism through a reading of the *puruṣārthas* in the performance titled *Puruṣārtthakkūttŭ* set in Kerala. The argument unravels as follows: the *puruṣārthas* are difficult to follow. In times of moral and ethical degeneration, it is even more difficult to act on the basis of their prescriptive ideals. Sensing the 'uniqueness of our current times',[65] the Brahmin Fool offers an alternative or substitute set of human aims: gluttony, kissing up to the King, enjoying prostitutes and cheating.[66] It is hoped that these will be easier to follow and act upon and will encourage people to do something rather than nothing just because following the original *puruṣārthas* seems so daunting.[67] The incommensurability of values is set between the Brahmin Fool and the Pious Brahmin, with the ideal always re-asserting itself and lurking behind in the shadows. *Hāsyārṇava* does not offer itself to this interpretation for reasons already mentioned above: it has no pious individuals restating the ideal or the norm.

Led primarily by the King and the brahmins, the *mūla* or root of ensuring order and dispensing punishment within the *Rājadharma-daṇḍanīti* framework, *Hāsyārṇava* illuminates a conscious and highly significant defiance of *varṇa* or the hierarchically arranged social classes. The vehicle for breaking *varṇa* rules and boundaries is the erotic element in the text. In employing the erotic in a radical subversion of the rules and rituals governing the social classes, *Hāsyārṇava* reiterates its status as a text that envisions disorder as the precondition for any concept of freedom in the Indic world. Recall yet again that the King addresses Inclined-Vulva as 'mother' and his visit to her house as equal to the merit of a hundred pilgrimages. But there are other more stark illustrations. Let us take the scene of a conversation between the brahmin Madanāndha-Miśra, Blind-with-Passion, and his brahmin disciple, Kulāla, Wild-Cock, to illustrate this point.

BLIND-WITH-PASSION: O Child! In whose house will we eat today?

WILD-COCK: O Good Sir! A procuress called Inclined-Vulva lives in this city. One hears she is hospitable and serves guests well. That is why we will eat at her place.

BLIND-WITH-PASSION: Is she well-born?

WILD-COCK: Is there any doubt? Even an outcaste from the lowest caste does not drink water in her house [caṇḍālo'pi asyā gṛhe pānīyaṁ na pibati].

BLIND-WITH-PASSION: (With enthusiasm) O Child! Then, let's go.

If we take a span of centuries, say, from the suggested dates of Manu's law codes between second century BCE and second century CE, to the fifteenth century CE text, *Daṇḍaviveka*[68] of Vardhamāna Upādhyāya, it is certain that, at least in theory, prostitutes were seen as the fifth caste. Questions of purity and impurity become paramount during this period. In dealing with the question of food unfit for a brahmin, Manu prohibits accepting food from a prostitute,[69] warning him that the food of a prostitute cuts him off from the worlds.[70] Skilled prostitutes were seen as thorns on the king's people's side and had to be removed.[71] Manu recommends death for a śūdra if he has sex with a guarded woman, and his limbs and wealth if he sleeps with an unguarded woman.[72] But for a brahmin having sex with a śūdra woman, he only levies a fine of 500 Paṇas, while sex with a lowest-born women invited a 1000 Paṇas fine. *Daṇḍaviveka* cites several authoritative *Dharmaṣāstra* sources[73] recommending death for cohabiting with low-caste women. Clearly, the relative institutionalised tolerance for the role of prostitutes seen in the *Arthaśāstra* was a thing of the past. To borrow Kesavan Veluthat's memorable phrase, they were no longer 'courtesans *de luxe*'[74] but caught in the spiral of caste purity and impurity. *Hāsyārṇava* subverts the consensus that Manu proposes and *Daṇḍaviveka* reaffirms.

★

There is one question that still remains unanswered: What makes *Hāsyārṇava* stand apart as a text, with celebration of disorder, chaos and transgression at its core? It has been argued that 'necessary but threatening disorder'[75] is an integral dimension of the brahminical Hindu idea of order. This leads to a relentless anxiety about creating boundaries, however fragile, and the fear of these boundaries being stormed by the proximate chaos. The brahmin ideal, therefore, attempts to transcend this fraught binary of order and disorder, among other things.[76] Also, though *dharma* in all its various meanings and dimensions unfolds in purposefully created order, its roots and, indeed, its motivation lie in the disorder that lies close at hand. Yet, there is also the view that it is wrong to assume that the *Dharmaṣāstras* are anything other than prescriptive accounts of an ideal society.[77] Not only would it be erroneous on our part to see a correspondence between them and actual life, but also to consign those trends, movements and ideas that deviate from the prescribed norms as 'unorthodox distortions' and 'sectarian developments'.[78] Does *Hāsyārṇava* belong to these obscure and neglected margins? Since there is so little known about the social and literary context of *Hāsyārṇava*, a few clues and hints from the text can help us reconstruct, however inadequately, the secret thread that probably binds the narrative.

Though convention demands that a new text begin with the writer invoking a preferred deity, and *Hāsyārṇava* is no exception, the opening verse depicts no expression of ordinary piety or reverence but reveals Lord Śiva and Pārvatī in impassioned sexual union. This erotic beginning spills over into the second verse too. Only in the third verse we hear the Sūtradhār, the principal male actor, tell us that the poet Jagadēśvara owes his poetic powers and his unstained family line to Lord Śiva. The first three verses resoundingly declare the tantric orientation of the text. After all, tantra conceives the world to be a manifestation of the erotic union of Śiva and Śakti, an alternative world that deviates from one proposed by the brahminical *Dharmaṣāstras* and their binaries. Neither division of the sexes nor *varṇa* categories are of any consequence in this denial of the normative social order and its ideals. When Tumour-of-Strife intones that 'Ultimate release is possible only when the supreme and incomparable Lord Śiva is propitiated with meat, fish and women', this formulation seems to place *Hāsyārṇava* firmly within the tantric universe.

Despite disclaimers to the contrary, tantra remains fundamentally misogynistic in its orientation.[79] But having acknowledged this undeniable fact, the focus on Streak-of-the-Young-Moon's-Crescent's body throughout the text too can be explained by understanding a tantric practice called the *kāmakalādhyāna*, which turns its focus on the female body, especially the breasts and genitalia.[80] Further, the brief reference in Act II to Vaiṣṇava devotion in the text is not necessarily a departure from the text's tantric moorings. Rather, it could allude to the early coming together of tantra and Vaiṣṇavism in Bengal leading to the formation of the Vaiṣṇava-Sahajiyā cult.[81] Another aspect of the text nudges us towards considering its tantric inspiration. This is Blind-with-Passion's response to being told that he has to perform a ritual fire-offering for the God of Love.

> The hollow of the loins of the fawn-eyed Streak will function as the altar for the sacrifice; near her loins is her vagina, that spot coveted by pleasure-loving men, which will act as the fire-pit; her breasts will act as the fruit meant for ritual offering. The excessively burning fire of amorous passion will act as the fire for the sacrifice; I will act as the officiating priest and my semen will be the material offered in the fire, while my penis will act as the wooden ladle, the sphya. Having these material that produce instant gratification in my possession, which man will forgo performing such an amorous sacrifice.

While the tantric universe and its ostensibly obscene language is what confines its ideas and rituals to the margins, such language and symbolism is not totally absent from texts that belong to the ancient orthodox tradition. This is what the Aitareya Brāhmaṇa, X, 3, 2–4, has to say:

> If, in the course of a recitation, the priest separates the first two quarters of a verse and brings the other two close together, this is because the woman separates her thighs and the man presses them during pairing; the priest thus represents pairing, so that the sacrifice will give numerous progeny.[82]

The *Bṛhadāraṇyaka Upaniṣad* says:

> A fire – that's what a woman is, Gautama. Her firewood is the Vulva; her smoke is the pubic hair; her flame is the vagina; when one penetrates her, that is her embers; and her sparks are like the climax. In that very fire gods offer semen, and from that offering springs a man.[83]

Put differently, while the orthodox and tantra texts may have near-identical passages, all erotic elements in tantra tend to be ritualistic. Kamil V. Zvelbil suggests[84] that the sexual realm is sanctified and homogenised in tantra with the help of myth and ritual, while myth and ritual are often elaborated in stark sexual terms. *Hāsyārṇava* consistently reflects this tantric element as well: the tantric theme is just another addition to many layers of meaning and significance that can be unearthed.

★

In all its fascinating complexity, *Hāsyārṇava* encourages us to look at the past with new eyes, if only because our sense of the past is increasingly inadequate, our sense of reality simplistic and we lack sense of the innumerable ironies, tensions, contradictions and paradoxes that fabricated our imperfect but colourful world. In acknowledging its undeniable richness, its neglect as text is also perplexing. Whether driven by a strong tantric undercurrent or by a conscious estrangement from the *Dharmaṣāstras* and their preferred world, it is a text that serves as a political satire for all times. In exhibiting defiance, it warns us that a mindless quest for order, efficiency, safety and comfort can only lead to violence, cruelty, inequality and injustice. By embracing estrangement from the ineluctable burden of a given reality, it offers the only way a messy, fragile and chaotic sense of freedom can be attained. But it also reveals a dimension of reality in a most unsuspecting fashion. It fails to resolve the conundrum of power. After all, we see every single boundary and all semblance of moral and ethical certainty dissolve in the course of the unfolding of its two acts. Law, legal procedure, boundaries of social classes and caste, ethics, morals, propriety, honour, chivalry, bravery, justice, empathy, truth, honesty—all these are rendered into a mighty heap of disorder and limitless chaos. Yet, despite this dissolution, not one individual abandons privilege and power. *Hāsyārṇava* shows that such a world is possible and may even exist. Doesn't the Mighty-Censurer say just that? That the death of creatures in this world is inevitable and this life is like a dream, and so one must not lament our sense of loss. But it is also a world where, to recall Ocean-of Deceit's memorable phrase, leeches live on the body of leeches. Some might call it a post-truth world today, but *Hāsyārṇava* prophetically predicted its logic many centuries back. And, hence, a political satire for all times.

Notes

1 Many readers of this essay introducing *Hāsyārṇava* have had one suggestion in common. It is a call to place the text within the *prahasana* tradition. I have consciously not done so because the purpose of this essay or the translation that follows is not a literary one. Neither is it Indological or philological. Even if such a comparison were to be done, the *Hāsyārṇava* would only compare to other *prahasanas* in a morphological sense. Just as the word *picaro* does not appear in *Lazarillo de Tormes*, the first picaresque work, and though the term is widely used to describe *Don Quixote*, Cervantes's classic

is not remotely picaresque. Similarly, this is an attempt to resurrect, privilege and interpret a neglected text, freeing it from its traditionally designated low position as a *prahasana* among the *rūpakas* of the Indian dramatic tradition (*Nāṭaka, Prakarṇa, Aṅka, Vyāyoga, Bhāṇa, Samavakāra, Vīthi, Prahasana, Ḍima, Īhamṛga* are the ten dramatic forms or *daśarūpa* listed in the *Nāṭyaśāstra*). If one is compelled to place *Hāsyārṇava* within the *prahasana* tradition, then it suffices to say that it is a mixed *prahasana* that borrows a few elements like Transference, Deception, Compliment, and Outvying from among the 13 types of *Vīthi*. In this reading, transcending the limits imposed by its form, *Hāsyārṇava*, emerges as a text that embodies a searing and unforgiving political and social commentary. It disrupts, disturbs and unsettles norms and interrogates established concepts and categories.

2 The *Arthaśāstra* of Kauṭilya clearly prescribes the time a king ought to spend in the women's quarters. See 1.20.1–23 in *King, Governance and Law in Ancient India: Kauṭilya's Arthaśāstra*, A New Annotated Translation by Patrick Olivelle, Oxford University Press, New Delhi, 2013, pp.94–95.

3 The *Kāma Sūtra* of Vātsyāyana has an entire section titled 'Paradārīka' (Other Men's Wives). See *The Complete Kāma Sūtra*, translated by Alain Daniélou, Inner Traditions India, Rochester, 1994, pp.309–376. See also, *The Law Codes of Manu*, A new translation by Patrick Olivelle, 8.352–363, Oxford University Press, Oxford and New York, 2009 imprint, p.149.

4 *Arthaśāstra*, 7.5.19–27, p.290.

5 The *Arthaśāstra* goes on to assert that "For this entire treatise boils down to the mastery over the senses." See, *Kauṭilya's Arthaśāstra*, 1.7. 1–4.

6 Monier Monier-Williams, *A Sanskrit-English Dictionary*, Motilal Banarsidass Publishers, Delhi, 1999 edition, p.26; Vaman Shivram Apte, *The Student's Sanskrit-English Dictionary*, Motilal Banarsidass Publishers, Delhi, 2000 edition, p.17.

7 Lee Siegel, *Laughing Matters: Comic Tradition in India*, The University of Chicago Press, Chicago and London, 1987, p.150.

8 David Dean Shulman, *The King and the Clown in South Indian Myth and Poetry*, Princeton University Press, Princeton, NJ, 1985, p.89.

9 For a fascinating discussion of the concept of rājadharma, see Mark McClish, 'King: Rājadharma' in *Hindu Law: A New History of Dharmaśāstra*, Edited by Patrick Olivelle and David R. Davis, Jr., Oxford University Press, New Delhi, 2018, pp.257–272.

10 Mark McClish, 'Legal Procedure: Vyavahāra', in *Hindu Law: A New History of Dharmaśāstra*, Edited by Patrick Olivelle and David R. Davis, Jr., Oxford University Press, New Delhi, 2018, pp.283–298. In Hāsyārṇava, the phrases indicatinga decline in following legal procedure are 'vyavahāro astaṁ' uttered by the Servant-Spy and 'avyavahāro jātaḥ' by Ocean-of-Disorder.

11 Brian K. Smith, *Classifying the Universe: The Ancient Indian Varna System and the Origins of Caste*, Oxford University Press, New York, 1994, pp.38–39.

12 'While exaggerated statements about the King and his power can be regularly found, these fall under the rubric of *arthvaada*: exaltations, exaggerated statements whose only purpose is to emphatically praise certain persons or objects, and which, therefore, are given a verbal expression which goes beyond the actual meaning they convey'. See, Ludo Rocher, *Studies in Hindu Law and Dharmashastra*, edited by Donald R. Davis, Jr, Anthem Press, London, 2012, p.352.

13 If he rejects the advice of the brahmins, he not only fails in his duty, but even incurs the risk of governing badly. See *The Law Code of Manu*, IX.67. See also, Robert Lingat, *The Classical Law of India*, Munshiram Manoharlal Publishers Pvt. Ltd., New Delhi, 1993, p.218.

14 Vaśiṣṭha, 1.39–41, in *A Dharma Reader: Classical Indian Law*, translated and edited by Patrick Olivelle, Permanent Black in association with Ashoka University, Ranikhet, 2016, p.67.

15 *Kauṭilya's Arthaśāstra*, 1.6.2–4, p.71.
16 Ibid., 1.7.2, p.72. Olivelle here translates Dharma as Law and Artha as Success.
17 *The Law Code of Manu*, 7.44–53, p.109. It is interesting that Manu includes music, singing and dancing in the list of vices emerging out of pleasure.
18 *Kauṭilya's Arthaśāstra*, 1.8, p.72.
19 Ibid., 1.11, pp.74–75.
20 *The Law Code of Manu*, 7.58–59, pp.134–135. The sixfold policy includes questions of war and peace, the condition of the kingdom, the kingdom's wealth and its protection and the consolidation of gains.
21 Viśvabhaṇḍa, Kalahānkura, Madanāndhamiśra, Kulāla, Mahānindaka, Mithyārṇava and Mahāyātrika.
22 Lingat, *The Classical Law of India*; Smith, *Classifying the Universe: The Ancient Indian Varna System and the Origins of Caste*; Rocher, *Studies in Hindu Law and Dharmashastra*; Donald R. Davis, Jr., *The Spirit of Hindu Law*, Cambridge University Press, New Delhi, 2010; Alf Hiltebeitel, *Dharma: Its Early History in Law, Religion and Narrative*, Oxford University Press, New York, 2011.
23 *Śatapatha Brāhmaṇa*, edited by A. Weber, Chowkhamba Sanskrit Series, Varanasi, 1964, 5.4.4.16–19.
24 Vasiṣtha, 1.39–41, in *A Dharma Reader: Classical Indian Law*, translated and edited by Patrick Olivelle, Permanent Black in association with Ashoka University, Ranikhet, 2016, p.186.
25 *Kauṭilya's Arthaśāstra*, 1.3.16–17, p.68.
26 *Dharmasūtras: The Law Codes of Ancient India*, A New Translation by Patrick Olivelle, Oxford University Press, 1999, pp.93–94.
27 Ibid., p.299.
28 'Brihadaranyaka Upanishad', 1.14, in *Upaniṣads*, A New Translation by Patrick Olivelle, Oxford University Press, 1998, p.16.
29 Rocher, *Studies in Hindu Law and Dharmashastra*, p.353.
30 McClish, 'King: Rājadharma', p.258.
31 Ibid., p.268.
32 *The Law Code of Manu*, 7.2–7, p.106.
33 *Dharmasūtras: The Law Codes of Ancient India*, Āpastamba, 2.10.6, p.53; Gautama, 10.7–8, pp.93–94; Vasiṣtha, 19.7–8, p.299.
34 The phrase 'accede to being used' is explained by Olivelle as:

> Different beings open themselves to being used (literally 'enjoyed') by others; one can think of the chain of food and eaters. In socio-political context, moreover, 'being used may refer specifically to the king's enjoyment of his subjects' wealth through taxes and duties.

The Law Code of Manu, pp.107, 262.
35 Ibid., 7.15; 7.17–18.
36 Rocher, *Studies in Hindu Law and Dharmashastra*, p.346.
37 Vaśiṣṭha, 19.48; Gautama, 14.45, in *Dharmasūtras: The Law Codes of Ancient India*, p.301; p.103; The Law Code of Manu, 5.93–98; 8.311, pp.91–92; p.146.
38 Hiltebeitel, *Dharma: Its Early History in Law, Religion and Narrative*, p.239.
39 Ibid., p.239.
40 *The Mahābhārata*, Volume 8, translated by Bibek Debroy, Penguin Books, Gurgaon, 2013, pp.171–172.
41 Ibid., pp.171–175.
42 *The Law Code of Manu*, 7.22–25, p.107.
43 Shulman, *The King and the Clown in South Indian Myth and Poetry*, pp.28–32.
44 Mark McClish, 'Punishment: Daṇḍa', in *Hindu Law: A New History of Dharmaśāstra*, Edited by Patrick Olivelle and David R. Davis, Jr., Oxford University Press, New Delhi, 2018, p.273.

45 Gavin Flood, 'The Meaning and Context of the *Puruṣārthas*', in *The Fruits of Our Desiring: An Enquiry into the ethics of the Bhagvadgītā*, Edited by Julius Lipner, Bayeux, Calgary, 1997, pp.11–27.
46 *The Law Code of Manu*, 7.27, p.107.
47 Charles Malamoud, 'On the Rhetoric and Semantics of Puruṣārtha', in *Way of Life: King, Householder, Renouncer, Essays in honour of Louis Dumont*, Edited by T.N. Madan, Motilal Banarsidass Publishers, Delhi, 1988 edition, pp.33–54.
48 Donald Davis Jr., 'Being Hindu or Being Human: A Reappraisal of the *Puruṣārthas*', *Journal of Hindu Studies*, Vol.8, No. 1/3 (Jan., 2004), pp.1–27.
49 Shulman, *The King and the Clown in South Indian Myth and Poetry*, p.90.
50 The order of the fish, *matsyanyaya*, flourishes, where the big fish eat the small fish.
51 *The Mahabharata*, p.171.
52 It will be part of another discussion whether individuals freeing themselves from the *dharma*-stranglehold can also emancipate themselves from the consequences of *karma*.
53 Kalidasa, *Kumarasambhavam: The Origin of the Young God*, translated by Hank Heifetz, Penguin Books, Gurgaon, 2017, pp.149–169.
54 *The Śiva-Purāṇa*, Part II, translated by a board of scholars, Motilal Banarsidass Publishers, Delhi, 2008 imprint, pp.540–544, 700–716.
55 See especially the verses of the third song in Part I of the poem. *The Gītagovind of Jayadeva: Love Song of the Dark Lord*, edited and translated by Barbara Stoler Miller, Motilal Banarsidass, Delhi, 1984, pp.74–76.
56 *The Complete Kāma Sūtra*, 6.2.13–14, p.407.
57 The young courtesan's conflict with her mother about the choice of lovers is part of the knowledge the *Kāma Sūtra* imparts. Ibid., 6.2.57–58, p.414.
58 *Kauṭilya's Arthaśāstra*, 1.20.20, p.95.
59 Ibid., 2.27.1–30, pp.158–160.
60 Ibid., 2.4.11, p.106.
61 Ibid., 3.13.37, p.210.
62 Ibid., 4.13.38, p.252.
63 *The Complete Kāma Sūtra*, 5.5.1; 5.5.28, p.365. In line with the *Arthaśāstra*, the *Kāma Sūtra* allows prostitutes to be invited to the palace, 5.5.13–21.
64 Donald R. Davis Jr., 'Satire as Apology: The *Puruṣārtthakkūttŭ* of Kerala', in *Irreverent History: Essays for M.G.S. Narayanan*, Edited by Kesavan Veluthat and Donald R. Davis, Jr., Primus Books, Delhi, 2014, pp.93–109.
65 Ibid., p.102.
66 Ibid., p.98.
67 Ibid., p.101.
68 *Daṇḍaviveka of Vardhamāna Upādhyāya*, translated into English by Dr. Bhabatosh Bhaṭṭāchārya, The Asiatic Society, Calcutta, 1973.
69 *The Law Code of Manu*, 4.209, p.80.
70 Ibid., 4.219, p.81.
71 Ibid., 9.259–260, p.174. The term used is 'kaṇṭaka-śodhana', literally meaning 'to root-out the thorns'.
72 Ibid., 8.374, p.150.
73 *Daṇḍaviveka of Vardhamāna Upādhyāya*, p.149.
74 Kesavan Veluthat, *Of Ubiquitous Heroines and Elusive Heroes: The Cultural Milieu of Medieval Maṇipravāḷa Kāvyas from Kerala*, ICHR, New Delhi, 2013, p.20.
75 David Shulman, 'The Enemy Within: Idealism and Dissent in South Indian Hinduism', in *Orthodoxy, Heterodoxy and Dissent in India*, Edited by S.N. Eisenstadt, Reuven Kahane and David Shulman, Mouton Publishers, Berlin, 1984, pp.17–18. See also, Federico Squarcini, '*Pāṣaṇḍin, vaitaṇḍika, vedanindaka* and *nāstika*. On Criticism, Dissenters and Polemics and the South Asian Struggle for the Semiotic Primacy of Veridiction', *Orientalia Suecana*, Vol. LX (2011), pp.101–115.
76 Ibid., p.18.

77 Friedhelm Hardy, 'Hinduism', in *Turning Points in Religious Studies. Essays in Honour of Geoffrey Parrinder*, Edited by U. King, T & T Clark, Edinburgh, 1990, p.147.
78 Ibid., p.147.
79 Douglas Renfrew Brooks, *The Secret of the Three Cities: An Introduction to Hindu Śākta Tantrism*, The University of Chicago Press, Chicago, 1990, pp.105–106.
80 Ibid., pp.81–82.
81 Edward C. Dimock, Jr., *The Place of the Hidden Moon: Erotic Mysticism in the Vaiṣṇava-sahajiyā Cult of Bengal*, The University of Chicago Press, Chicago, 1989, pp.35–37.
82 Kamil V. Zvelebil, *The Poets of the Powers: Freedom, Magic, and Renewal*, Integral Publishing, California, 1993, p.47.
83 Brihadaranyaka Upanishad', 6.2.13, in *Upaniṣads*, A New Translation by Patrick Olivelle, Oxford University Press, 1998, p.83.
84 Zvelebil, *The Poets of the Powers: Freedom, Magic, and Renewal*, p.47.

2

A NOTE ON THE TEXT AND THE TRANSLATION

A dissonant and unsettling text like *Hāsyārṇava* ought to have had better visibility. Yet, very little is known about either its literary history or its author. We know that it was composed by a poet called Jagadēśvara Bhaṭṭāchārya. The text tells us that he was from an impeccable lineage; whether it was caste lineage or poetic lineage, we do not know. What about the text itself? It is also normal for the date or year of composition of many ancient or medieval texts to be the subject of intense speculation and conjecture. *Hāsyārṇava* falls into this category.

While there is scant reference to the text among commentators, they have either remained silent of the question of its historical context or given dates that widely differ. Calling it a `medieval satire' has been adequate for those not wanting to hazard a guess regarding the period of its composition. Lee Siegel's[1] substantial survey of the comic traditions in India fails to mention the text's provenance, and so does an earlier history of Sanskrit drama by A. Berriedale Olith.[2] David Shulman[3] places it in the fourteenth century, and the only other extant translation in English by Ram Dayal Munda[4] and David Nelson too concurs with the fourteenth-century date.

The other usual signs within a text used as internal evidence to date a text are unavailable to us. There are no references to Muslims, Jesuits, gunpowder, local gods and goddesses, folk or tribal traditions. Neither are these markers reliable tools to establish the historicity of a text. It is well known that brahmins continued to write poetry and prose in Sanskrit almost till the nineteenth century inhabiting an altogether different temporality, ignoring historical events with benign condescension.

Part of the story of its neglect has to do with a certain nineteenth-century view of Sanskrit literature driven by European Indology and Orientalism. This was a view that promoted a highly romanticised vision of India driven by simple life, mysticism and harmony between humans and nature, evidence of which was to be found in Kālidāsa's *Śakuntalā*. At the same time, most Indologists of that time found Indian spiritual life irrational and Hindu sects and philosophical doctrines superstitious and deficient. A text like *Hāsyārṇava* for them would have been an abomination, if not a curiosity. Though composed by a brahmin in Sanskrit, interspersed with dialogue in Prākṛta, it is a text that distances itself from transcendence, detachment and questions of purity and impurity. It celebrates blood and ritual sexuality, themes that hardly are the fodder for the idealistic, elite and sanctimonious brahmins and Indologists alike of that period.

These nineteenth-century sentiments are reflected in Kali Kumar Datta Shastri's reading of *Hāsyārṇava* as a grossly indelicate satire written to underscore the licentiousness of brahmins masquerading as religious mendicants.[5] Even by nineteenth-century inspired standards, this reading is far off the mark, but so is Datta Shastri placing the composition of the text in the mid eighteenth-century Bengal. This periodisation is plainly incorrect. And there are compelling reasons to argue that *Hāsyārṇava* was composed much earlier than the eighteenth century.

The *Gītagovind* of Jayadeva establishes Vaishnavism in its literary form in Bengal by the end of the twelfth century. It brings a certain erotic mysticism to Vaishnavism, which existed from Jayadeva's period to the time of Caitanya in the late fifteenth and early sixteenth centuries. In its evolution, it existed along with numerous trantric cults like the Nāth and the Sahajiyā. Orthodox sects like the Shaivites and the Vaishnavites had to contend with tantric cultic modes of privileging the erotic and the sensuous as a way to salvation. It was also a period of the 'social tyranny of dominant Brahmanism with its protective, but despotic spirit'.[6] It has already been pointed out in the Introduction that *Hāsyārṇava* draws upon poetic inheritances as varied as the purāṇas, the kāvyas of Kālidāsa and the *Gītagovind* of Jayadeva, among others. But when it invokes Vaishnavism, it certainly does not seem to be that of the one Caitanya propagated: there is surprisingly little emphasis in a transgressive text like *Hāsyārṇava* on song and dance, though, most significantly, nāma-kīrtana, chanting of Kṛṣna's name, is mentioned once in Verse 10 of Act II.

All this is still merely circumstantial and speculative. Evidence of the text being older than eighteenth century comes from an unexpected source. In her study of the Nauṭankī theatre in North India, Kathryn Hansen[7] mentions *Hāsyārṇava* as the first *svāṅg* text in Braj Bhasha, composed between 1686 and 1689 by Rasrup. Is this the same *Hāsyārṇava* or just the same nomenclature for an entirely different text? Drawing upon Ram Narayan Agraval's work, Hansen points to internal evidence[8] that indicates that *Hāsyārṇava* was transcribed after a *naṭ* named Kamrup performed it before a king of Telangana. To clinch the argument that it is indeed the same *Hāsyārṇava*, now disseminated and performed in many regions of medieval India, the Ramrup text alludes to Kamrup mentioning King Anayasindhu in his performance.

It is now safe to say that *Hāsyārṇava* could have been composed any time between the fourteenth and seventeenth centuries. While the text translated here has an author called Jagadēśvara Bhaṭṭāchārya, there is little guarantee that he might have been the single author of this text. In being transcribed, performed and translated, we would have to assume that there were more than one version of the text and the content would have gone through the normal process of endless interpolations.

In translating the text, I have relied on the 1987 edition reprinted by Chaukhamba Sanskrit Pratishthan.[9] I have also compared it with the 1896 edition edited and published in Calcutta by Srinatha Vedantavagisha.[10] Both versions have errors and omissions, though the Chowkhamba version is more complete and reliable. While translating the text, I have avoided the flattening effects of a literal translation. While the translation stays loyal to the text, the translation expands and elaborates in order to capture a little of the original's sparkling quality and unsettling energy. And I have not forgotten that every effort in translating is also an act of interpretation.

Notes

1 Lee Siegel, *Laughing Matters: Comic Tradition in India*, The University of Chicago Press, Chicago and London, 1987.
2 A. Berriedale Olith, *The Sanskrit Drama in Its Origin, Development, Theory and Practice*, Oxford University Press, London, 1924.
3 David Dean Shulman, *The King and the Clown in South Indian Myth and Poetry*, Princeton University Press, Princeton, NJ, 1985, p.89.
4 *Jagadēśvara Bhaṭṭāchārya's One-Act Farce Hāsyārṇava: The Ocean of Laughter*, Translated from the Sanskrit by Ram Dayal Munda and David Nelson, Writers Workshop, Calcutta, 1976.
5 Kali Kumar Datta Shastri, *Bengal's Contributions to Sanskrit Literature*, Sanskrit College, Calcutta, 1974, p.22.
6 Sushil Kumar De, *The Early History of the Vaishnava Faith and Movement in Bengal*, Firma K.L. Mukhopadhyay, Calcutta, 1961, p.28.
7 Kathryn Hansen, *Grounds for Play: The Nauṭankī Theatre of North India*, Manohar, New Delhi, 1992, p.62.
8 Ibid., p.314.
9 *Hāsyārṇava Prahasana of Sri Jagadishwara Bhattacharya*, edited with the 'Prabha Hindi Commentary by Ishwar Prasad Chaturvedi, Chowkhamba Vidyabhawan, Varanasi, 1987.
10 *Hasyarnaba: A Drama in Two Acts by Jagdishwara Bhattacharya*, Edited and published by Shrinatha Vedantabagisha, Calcutta Press, Calcutta, 1896.

'Bandhurā' by Asma Menon.

3

NAME OF CHARACTERS IN *HĀSYĀRṆAVA* IN ORDER OF APPEARANCE

Sūtradhāra	Principal male actor
Naṭī	Principal female actor
King Anayasindhu	Ocean-of-Disorder
Servant	Spy
Kumativarmā	Protector-of-Folly
Bandhurā	Inclined-Vulva
Mṛgāṅkalekhā	Streak-of-the-Young Moon's-Crescent
Viśvabhaṇḍa	World-Buffoon
Kalahānkura	Tumor-of-Strife
Vyādhisindhu	Ocean-of-Diseases
Āturāntaka	Death-of-the-Afflicted
Raktakallol	Joy-in-Blood
Mithyārṇava	Ocean-of-Deceit
Sādhuhiṁsaka	Tormentor-of-Righteous
Raṇajambuka	Jackal-of-War
Mahāyātrika	Predictor-of-the-Great-Beyond
Madanāndhamiśra	Blind-with-Passion
Kulāla	Wild-Cock
Mahānindaka	Mighty-Censurer

4

ENGLISH TRANSLATION OF *HĀSYĀRṆAVA-PRAHASANAṀ*

Translated in English

Act 1

Bound together by vine-like arms in sexual union, their exertion makes the unctuous sandal on their bodies gather with the streaming perspiration.
The memory of sexual pleasure is summoned with a sense of amazement, with lips closely pressed, the breath rising, unsteadily.
Drawing in breath that makes a sound expressing sudden pleasure, eyes illuminated by delight, the hair on her body bristling with rapture, her reeling eyebrows and her hands performing a whirling dance.
The joy and emotion of love in Śiva and Pārvatī's impassioned sexual union spreads and scatters all around. (1)

'Rāhu, the demon of the sky, is on his course from the sun to the moon, wanting to go after the moon, longing to swallow it for nourishment, causing an eclipse.
O Moon-faced Pārvatī ! Wonder if he should not be confounded by your face that resembles the sparkle of the moon and desires to seize and eat it?'
Pārvatī, hearing her Lord speak, starts to gaze at the sky to follow Rāhu's trajectory, while Śiva intensely kisses revered Pārvatī's mouth. Let this eulogy for Lord Trinayana fulfil the desires of good and virtuous men. (2)

After the benedictory verses had been recited, the Sūtradhāra, the Principal male actor, said:
It is meaningless to elaborate excessively, thus:

Poet Jagadēśvara Bhaṭṭāchārya's poem is like a fair-complexioned and remarkable woman, who is free, spontaneous, self-willed and capable of generating wild emotions;

this poem is adorned with the rules of poetics such as the ideal standards of comparison and analogy that help arrive at correct knowledge;
it is pure from the perspective of grammar and other stringent standards;
it is replete with rasās like humour and capable of producing mirth; listening to poet Jagadēśvara's poem, the teeth of the discerning seem as if falling out;
Its charm delights the soul spirit of the discerning and it brings them great joy. (3)

He, whose worship of Lord Śiva made his lineage unstained and illuminated his poetic powers, that poet, Shri Jagadēśvara, ordered me: 'Befitting the spring season, you must produce joy in the hearts of those who savour and appreciate poetry by performing my prahasana titled Hāsyārṇava'.

Certainly, this order of his has to be carried out. In this assembly of discerning people, my heart too is impatient and eager to luxuriate in the spring using my charming voice to flirt, and also to dance. Therefore, let me begin dancing, playing instruments and singing. (Turns and looks around) Oh! The beauty of spring agitates and fills my heart because—

Which sensitive human heart does not get excited with joy in the spring when the breeze, touched by the Malaya forest, brings a waft of sandal-infused fragrance, on hearing the sweet humming of nectar-intoxicated bees and listening to the sweet song of the cuckoo? (4)

Additionally,

In the time of spring these days, what a bee intoxicated with drinking nectar not do? The bee roams buzzing in the midst of gardens, flies in the direction of the sky, and then falls yet again from the sky. Walking around with its pollen-smeared body and darting glances around, it kisses flowers and embraces his beloved. (5)

O Lady, the pupils of your eyes cast flirtatious sidelong glances like a bunch of lotuses playfully dangling from a golden vase.

How can there be pleasure, then, without a woman? (Turns, and facing the tiring room behind the curtains, he reads)—

O Lady, The pupils of your eyes cast flirtatious side-long glances like a bunch of lotuses playfully dangling from a golden vase!
Your body resembles the rays of the moon!
You are like the arrows of Kāmadeva, the God of Love!
Your body resembles nectar as if bitten by the snake-like God of Love!
You are shrewd, clever, sharp! You are agreeable and resplendent! Beloved! Come here fast! (6)

(The Naṭī, the principal female actor, enters)

O Husband! I have presented myself as per your wishes. Therefore, please favour me with your kind words.

Principal Male Actor : O Revered Lady! Look—

When the sweet strains of the cuckoo's singing are spreading in all directions, when bees are intently kissing the flowers in the arbour;
touched by the Malaya-forest breeze, the fragrance of jasmine flowers is wafting all around—
With the appearance of spring, which discerning person is not afflicted by the arrows of the God of Love? (7)

Additionally:

In this spring-time, the vines of the Mādhavikā creeper, laden with newly blooming flowers are embracing the mango tree with joy.
Through the unmanifest sound of this joyful embrace but also because of the sweet singing of the cuckoo, the Mādhavikā vines seem instructing a newly-wed bride in the art of making love. (8)

Principal Female Actor : (Feigns absent-minded indifference)
Principal Male Actor : O revered lady! Why do you seem absent-minded?
Principal Female Actor : O Husband, have you not heard?
Principal Male Actor : What?
Principal Female Actor : I am preoccupied and absent-minded because I have to discuss matters of governance with a King called Anayasindhu, Ocean-of-Disorder, who invariably confines himself in the women's quarter of his palace.
Principal Male Actor : O beloved! Is this true?
Principal Female Actor : Indeed, it is.

(Voice from the wings is heard)

The King, Anayasindhu, Ocean-of-Disorder, is soon arriving with the intention of ascertaining the welfare as well as the misfortunes of this city.
People! Collect together and line up large waterless earthen pots and order the casting of lines with needles of grain husk along the main street. (9)

Principal Male Actor : Looks up at the sky and listens. After hearing—

Dread and apprehension has driven law [nītī] itself and all righteous people to speedily flee to a far-off destination. Who has not noticed the crafty speech of cheats and frauds, devoted entirely to defrauding the wealth of others?
In what prevails in the Kingdom today, who does not take by force another man's wife to gratify his own lust?
This King now approaches the city, and, hence, O Beloved, it does not seem right for us to stay here. (10)

Therefore, let us both take this way and go elsewhere.

(The Sūtradhār and the Naṭī both exit.)
(End of the Prologue)

(Thereafter, King Anayasindhu, Ocean-of-Disorder, enters with a servant)

King : (To himself) Ah! It is a matter of great regret that my body is worn-out because of the attack of the flowery arrows of the God of Love, leaving my body consumed by the fire of amorous love; day and night I think of ways to have sex with wives of other men. This is the reason why for a long time now I have not been able to inquire into the affairs of the people of the city.

(Emerges into the light and speaks to the Servant-Spy) Ah, Supreme Spy! O Expounder-of-False-Perceptions! Investigate completely the state of my kingdom.

Servant-Spy : Whatever my Lord commands.

(After saying this, the spy comes out, looks ahead and then re-enters to speak in a high-pitched voice in the King's ear) O Lord! I have unravelled the mysteries of the kingdom.

King : Tell, tell.

Servant-Spy : The Kingdom's legal procedure and civil law [vyavahāra] have completely declined and have been set aside because of lack of consultation for a very long time.

King : (With anger) How?

Servant-Spy : (Speaking in Sanskrit) Lord! Because—

All men have left the wives of other men and embrace only their wives; despite presence of clusters of well-born and learned brahmins, it is the cobbler who mends shoes.
Shameless people worship brahmins despite the secure existence of the lowest castes.
Oh King! This kind of extreme transgression of rules has arisen in your kingdom. (11)

Additionally,

Women apply collyrium to their eyes rather than to their loins, do not apply collyrium to the parting of the hair on the forehead where, instead, vermillion is adorned and shines with radiance. They wear their anklets on their feet and smear the soles of their feet with red lac instead of painting their eyes with it. They adorn the jeweled necklace on both their breasts and not on their feet. They wear the golden girdle around the circumference of their hips and loins and not on their lips.
With great pain, I have seen such a confused and nonsensical way of wearing jewellery in every house in the kingdom. (12)

King : (Listens to spy, and, then, speaks to himself)

For a long time, I have not thought and deliberated little about issues concerning the kingdom. This has hastened the decline of all legal procedure. Okay, I am going to prescribe punishments.
(Comes into light)
Hear, call a minister called Kumativarmā, Protector-of-Folly.
Servant-Spy : Whatever my Lord commands.
(He exits and re-enters with the minister)
Protector-of-Folly enters and greets the King with his left hand.
Folly : Without being asked for my consent, oh Lord, you can clearly command what you want me to execute.
King : O Minister! In the absence of a suitable place to hold court, I have not for long been able to converse about the affairs of the state.
Folly : (Surprised)
My Lord! Right here there is an extremely delightful place to hold court.
King : Please tell, please tell!
Folly : The house of a procuress call Badhurā, Inclined-Vulva.
King : (Laughing loudly)
Protector-of-Folly! It seems as if you consulted with my heart's innermost desire before entering the court. Disinclined to touch the Queen's sagging breasts, it is my desire too that I embrace a prostitute. Can the God of Love ever reside in women with breasts that droop to touch their navel?

Also,

Beholding the lofty breasts of agreeable women, breasts that rise like an inaccessible mountain fortress, the God of Love forcibly tears the hearts of young men with very sharp arrows of women's sidelong glances.
Meanwhile, in this war of amorous passion, the God of Love's advances bruise the breasts and bring about their downfall. Once the fort begins to fall, the cowardly and timid God of Love begins to retreat and run away—this is my belief. (13)

Folly : Shall we go?
King : (Goes happily with the minister)
Servant Spy : O Lord! The fragrance of camphor, sandal, deer-musk and various flowers is coming from this direction. Therefore, I guess this must be Inclined-Vulva's house. O Lord! Please come this way.
King : (Entering, he says joyously) This, then, is Inclined-Vulva's house. Coming here, I have attained the merit of a hundred pilgrimages.
Folly : Where is the procuress Inclined-Vulva?

(After this, Inclined-Vulva enters, happily surrounded by a hundred paramours)

Vulva : Oh! Surprise! Surprise! Hear, O paramours! The universal monarch among the roguish, King Ocean-of-Disorder, has arrived; so you should not delay singing spring-related songs, with cymbals and drums as accompaniments.

(All the paramours come closer, and sing happily)

Filled with the sweetest singing of nectar-intoxicated bees, accompanied with the songs of women with extremely beautiful voices, crowded with young men whose hearts have been pierced open by the God of Love—May all these make the season of spring pleasurable for you. (14)

(They repeatedly sing and play in this manner)

King : (He listens, and then whispers in the minister's ear) Oh! Protector-of-Folly, Vulva desires something.

Folly : You are the greatest sinner in the entire world. Therefore, sparing everyone else, lightening will strike only your head.

King : I do not know what will happen. But what should I do now?

Folly : Having demonstrated your meanness, you must undertake three fasts in this pilgrim spot, comprising abstinence from all sensual gratification.

King : (To himself) Enough of being alarmed. Let me greet Vulva in order to deceive her. (In the light) Mother Vulva! I offer my obeisance to you.

Vulva : May Mṛgāṅkalekhā, Streak-of-the-Young Moon's-Crescent be pleased with you.

King : (Delighted, says to himself) This procuress, Vulva, has not asked me for any favours, and so I have been freed of the fear of committing a great sin. (In the light) Where is the Streak-of-the-Young-Moon's-Crescent?

(After this, Streak-of-the-Young-Moon's-Crescent, her vine-like body decorated with special jewellery, enters)

Streak : O Mother! Who is this?

Vulva : O Daughter! You don't know him? King Ocean-Of-Disorder has come to seek an audience with you.

Streak : (Smiling) What could be more meritorious than that?

King : (Looking at Streak) She has an amazing body-

Her face beats the lustre of the moon, her tremulous eyes are darkened with collyrium, she expresses herself by rotating her eyebrows that resemble a vine, her forehead adorns an ornamental mark made of sandal infused with deer-musk. Her beautiful lips are red like the colour of the Bandhuka flower: even gods and sages can get infatuated hearing her nectar-laced speech. Who would not find agreeable such a beautiful body that is like a lotus unlikely to be found in all the three worlds? (15)

Additionally,

Her body is like a fine lake, her resplendent youth is like the water, her face seems like a lotus amidst the mire of deer-musk, her hands are like lotus stalks, while her swerving eyes resemble the whirling of bees. Her breasts are like two rival elephants; my mind wants to angrily crush her breast-elephants, but how can this mind rise and leave the lake that is Streak-of-the-Young-Moon's-Crescent's body? (16)

(After saying this, he finds the Vulva distracted, and says)
O Vulva! Why do you seem so absent-minded?

Vulva : My Lord! I am getting distracted because I am awaiting the arrival of a paid preceptor [upādhyāya] called Viśvabhaṇḍa, World-Buffoon. He is coming to instruct Streak in the science of love-making.

King : (With joy) The World-Buffoon is also our family priest.

(Voice from the Wings)

He fasts during the day but eats fish and flesh at night, he sports the matted hair of an ascetic but keenly desires whoring.
He, who is the crest-jewel of the perfidious, wearing ochre robes and holding an elegant staff, the revered World-Buffoon is winding his way here. (17)

(After this, the World-Buffoon enters with a student, Kalahānkura, Tumor-of-Strife.)

Buffoon : (He circumambulates the place, looks ahead and speaks)
I say! This is the beautiful time of spring.
And, also

The sweet-smelling and intoxicating fragrance of the spring makes hearts of the amorous drunk with passion. It is a companion to the God of Love, a brother to one who seeks gratification, a destination where a variety of gestures that suggest pleasure, coquetry, wantonness and coyness come together and abound. (18)

(Looks at the student and reads)

The notes of cymbals made of bell-metal and of drums are reverberating across the entire sky. The soft but incessant sound of the mṛdaṅg playing is also getting diffused in all directions.

The fragrance of camphor, aloe wood and sandal has infused the air and pervades all the quarters of the sky;
My dear child! Go and swiftly find out the person in whose house such festivities are being celebrated. (19)

Tumour : (circumambulates and says)
O Lord! The festivities are at the procuress called Inclined-Vulva's home.

World-Buffoon : (With joy) My child! Last year, Inclined-Vulva, the procuress, had invited us to a meal. Hence, this occasion seems appropriate.

(After another circumambulation, they enter Inclined-Vulva's porch)

Vulva : Preceptor! This is a broken seat. Revered Sir, please sit on it.

Buffoon : (Pretends to sit and says with reverence) Mother Vulva! I bow to you.

Vulva : Son! May you swim across the ocean of libido.

Buffoon : (Looking at Streak)
If I manage to hold the large jar-like breasts of this deer-eyed girl, then I will be able to swim across the ocean of libido. (20)

Streak : (Smiling, looks at the World-Buffoon)

King : (To himself) This is the World-Buffoon, the great preceptor. He has already received the blessings of Vulva, the procuress worshipped by the entire body of prostitutes; he continues to sit with her in order to obtain more blessings.
(In the light) O Lord! I bow to you.

Buffoon : Hear, Tumour-of-Strife! You must swiftly pronounce a benediction for the King.

Tumour : (Laughing loudly, he rubs hemp and the sacred Dūrvā grass together, collects rice and intones loudly in Sanskrit)
May menstrual discharge appear from your eyes.

Additionally,

May your enemies grow, let your fears increase, may your ailments grow, let your debts and sins enlarge. May you attain the prosperity of misfortune and stupidity—may you attain these seven prosperities. (21) (Intones the benediction and sprinkles Dūrvā grass and rice over the King's head)

King : O Lord! Who is this depraved lad?

Buffoon : You do not know him

He is the fire that has consumed his entire clan, he is the ultimate embodiment of terrible sins, he is the cumulation of all carelessness.
He is heroic when it comes to robbing people of their money, he embodies folly and is cruel—this is Tumour-of-Strife. (22)

(Speaks while looking towards Inclined-Vulva)

O child! Tumour-of-Strife!

Her pendulous breasts are like low-hanging water-laden clouds, old age has rendered her like arable land that is destroyed, she is now the seat of all sorts of diseases; like flamingos departing, the ornaments in her ankles are no longer there, she is blind like a star having lost its lustre.
Her advanced years make people disregard her as an object of desire the way the face of the moon gets concealed. This is Inclined-Vulva. These days, looking at her suddenly reminds one of an unpleasant floating cloud. (23)

My child! Please go to the revered Inclined-Vulva and pay your respects to her.

Tumour : (Dances around with great glee and prostrates between Inclined-Vulva's legs. He, then, looks up the hollow space between her loins, claps his hands and laughing uproariously, speaks in Sanskrit)

Oh! Great Preceptor! It is amazing that this
Inclined-Vulva has a beard underneath her face.

Additionally,

After beholding the ravages of old age, fear has shrivelled-up her cunt. (24)

Vulva : (Smiling) This brahmachārī is very corrupt. Hence, he justifies the name Kalahānkura, Tumour-of-Strife.

Buffoon : (Looking at Streak)
Wonderful! How intense are this young girl's amorous gestures.

Self-willed and unrestrained, she looks and smiles; after sufficient leisure, she pauses, and then yawns, and, with that, her whole body quivers.
She prolongs the moment of rapture, while the cloth covering the slope of her breasts slips and falls on all sides.
Untying and loosening her hair, embracing her companions, she implores an answer from her companion without even having asked a question;
Who is this exquisite woman with tremulous eyes who shines when it comes to the amorous pastime of making love. (25)

Furthermore

Eyes that are playful like the wag-tail's eyes, a face beautiful like a golden lotus, full and erect breasts that are constantly tremulous.
She has a slender waist and her hips are swollen and abundant;
If Lord Shiva, the Great Ascetic, looks at Streak even once, will he too not be wounded by the arrows of the God of Love? (26)

Vulva : O Preceptor! My daughter, Streak, is now adequately prepared to study the science of love-making.

Buffoon : (Laughing) At this juncture, my school too is bereft of students.

Streak : O Mother! His nails and teeth are old and decayed like that of an ageing tiger; old age has transformed him into a mere bag of skin and bones; but day and night, this shameless World-Buffoon derisively laughs at me and ridicules me.

Tumour : (In anger) O Vile Prostitute! One who seizes other people's sons and their wealth! Don't look at my teacher and surmise that he has fallen among bad company; after all, his wife, despite making love to him constantly, ceaselessly wanders around seeking great practitioners of the science of love-making in order to enhance her knowledge of this science. Such is her devotion to her husband that she puts on a widow's attire and pretends to be ready to follow the World-Buffoon to his pyre and immolate herself after her husband is gone. You still dare call our preceptor old? Apart from this, our preceptor still sheds clothes that cover his shame and sleeps in the lap of his mother—and you still call such a preceptor shameless?

(Pretends to be angry)

Streak : (Laughing) That brahmin woman is blessed, the brahmin disciple is blessed, and so is this brahmin preceptor.

Vulva : O daughter! You must not say such nasty things. You have not got to know the preceptor well till now. Though the World-Buffoon is the preceptor of all rogues and he is old, he can illuminate sexual love the same way the sun illuminates the blossoming of a lotus.

Buffoon : (Listens, and speaks to himself) Oh! What a surprise—

Inclined-Vulva's mop of white hair on her head and her white eyebrows are like the Kāśa flower open in all its glory; all her teeth have fallen out because of old age.
Decrepitude has rendered her body, once the abode of amorous love, emaciated; her breasts have shrivelled and hang down. Despite such a transformation, listening to her voice still rouses feelings of amorous desire. (27)

Anyway, where is she likely to vanish?

(In front of everyone, coming into the light) O Inclined-Vulva! You seem to be shaking a bit because of old age?

Vulva	:	This is true. Recalling the libertines loyally devoted to me in the past and their good qualities, I am now afflicted by the fever of amorous love.
Buffoon	:	(Laughing) O King! Vulva has been afflicted by the fever of amorous love.
King	:	Why don't you, then, call the great physician, Vyādhisindhu, Ocean-of-Diseases, the son of Āturāntaka, Death-of-the-Afflicted?
Buffoon	:	Are you not familiar with Death-of-the-Afflicted's son? Don't you know anything of his qualities?
King	:	Are you unfamiliar with the courtesy with which Ocean-of-Diseases instructs his patients?

For extreme pain in the stomach, apply a heated rod in the eyes;
for swelling of the feet, bore a hole in the soles of the feet;
for stone in the bladder, surgery must be performed inside the nose with a very sharp knife;
for gout and rheumatism, the patient must be made to drink hot oil.
For heart disease, the scrotum must be placed in the middle of an instrument made of two sticks and pressed hard.
When administered such pleasant forms of healing, which patient will not head towards the cremation ground? (28)

Additionally,

If suffering from cough, the patient must be made to inhale the smoke of burning husk;
if the patient's body has excess of flatulence, he must be made to labour, given purgatives and made to fast;
if suffering from weak digestion, the patient must be fed minced meat with his food;
if the patient is asthmatic, he ought to be continuously made to drink water.
If the patient complains of bile, he must be fed a gruel of dry ginger, holy fig-tree leaves, and chillies;
if there is fever caused by the disorder of bodily humours, the patient must be bathed inside a tub;
To what extent can one praise the sterling qualities of Ocean-of-Diseases, the Great Physician!

It is impossible for one mouth to adequately recite the list of his virtues. (29)

(From the wings)

He who kills every patient—the Royal Physician, Ocean-of-Diseases, is arriving on the stage;
The flesh on his feet is rotting in the extreme and small, round lumps have formed on them;
With the help of the front part of his garment, he frequently swats the flies settling on his bleeding sores; the intensity of his cough and its sound pervades all directions and resounds in the skies as well. (30)

(Ocean-of-Diseases enters, turns slowly, and speaks with great pride)

Diseases : *As a physician, all diseases are well-grounded in me; my disrepute and infamy are my glory.*
After being treated by me, even the immortal Mārkaṇḍeya cannot come back to life any time soon. (31)

Additionally,

The patient neither requires medicines nor treatment of any kind.
A mere glimpse of me is adequate for the person to die. (32)

Diseases : (Coming close) O Great Preceptor! I offer my salutations to you.

Buffoon : O Tumour-of-Strife! Confer blessings on the Royal Physician.

Tumour : (Raises his hand gesturing blessings and says loudly)
May you live with your enemies all your life,
May your life be short,
May you not live even for another two auspiciously designated moments,
May a sharp thorn pierce your heart,
May a snake bite your throat,
May the King decapitate you as punishment for the crimes of others,
May you always remain anxious about obtaining food,
And, may your house be constantly on fire. (33)

Diseases : Vile boy! You scorn at me?

Buffoon : (Laughing) O Diseases! Hope Death-of-the-Afflicted, your dead father, is well?

Diseases : How can he be well without a glimpse of you?
(Looking towards Streak)

Who in this entire world would not have his heart filled with covetousness at the sight of her breasts resembling gold jars? (34)

Buffoon : O Great Physician! I want to discuss with you some medicine-related matters.

Diseases : (With pride)

After having collected the rice and sesame seeds for cooking oblations for the ancestors,
after having picked a handsome axe in order to make a pyre,
Am I, the Physician, to be consulted immediately after the patient's family and relatives have given up all love for him from their hearts? (35)

Buffoon : (Laughing) You are a great physician. (Again laughing)

O Mighty Physician! Inclined-Vulva suffers from phlegm because of excessive indulgence in amorous love. That is why you must suggest her a cure.

Diseases : Why hasn't a concoction that has well-heated fatty oil not yet been irrigated into her anus? Now, do not delay this procedure.

Vulva : (Laughing, says to herself)

This physician is mindless.

(In the light) O Lord! Fortuitously, I have already encountered the foremost among great physicians.

Buffoon : (Looks towards the sky and speaks)

Ah! Having to attend to a thousand things, I have forgotten the question. (Laughing) O child, Kalahānkura! Remind me of the question to the physician.

Tumour : (Bursting into speech)

O Great Physician! Streak has developed an itch because of excessive application of vermillion and deer-musk on her body. So, please suggest what is to be done to cure this affliction.

Vulva : (Smiling, says to herself)

The student is just like his teacher. Dogs must, after all, live in a heap of ashes.

Diseases : *Apply an ointment of water-cabbage mixed with scorpion and fine dust the shape of thorns on all parts of Streak's body; this will eliminate the itch quickly. (36)*

Vulva : The medicine is good.

Tumour : (Pretending to think)

Yes, I remember now. Mighty Physician!

Inclined-Vulva has been suffering from a headache because of enjoying the battle of love. What needs to be done about it?

Vulva : (Smiling, coming closer)

O Great Physician! Though I am already familiar with your erudition, do please prescribe a medicine to cure my phlegm.

Diseases : (Thinks for a moment)
Hee! Hee! Why don't you say you are afflicted with phlegm?
Once, long ago, a reigning King suffering from extreme flatulence eventually developed phlegm. That time, Āturāntaka, Death-of-the-Afflicted, my father, who was an authority in the Ayurvedic texts of Caraka, Suśruta, Vāgbhaṭa and Nāgārjuna—he cured the King's phlegm by cleaning his eyes with black salt powder and applying one hundred leeches on the eyes.

Vulva : What should be done about my ailment?

Diseases : If a minor treatment is more effective, what, then is the use of prescribing an elaborate treatment—

Your phlegm will be destroyed if you insert insects like wasps, leeches and scorpion inside your nose and inside your eyes. (37)

Vulva : (Laughing) You are truly the son of Āturāntaka, Death-of-the-Afflicted.
(Commotion heard from the wings)

King : (Listens with ear towards the sky and, after listening, comes into the light)
Listen! Door-keeper! Find out who has come to meet me immediately. Bring him here fast.

Door-keeper : (Enters): Whatever My Lord wishes. (Goes out, looks properly, re-enters)
O Great King! Raktakallol, Joy-in-Blood, a barber, dragged by his garments by a bleeding resident of the city, is here.

King : Ask him to enter and present himself.

Door-keeper : (Goes out and re-enters)
O Great King! I present to you the barber who goes by the name Joy-in-Blood.

(Joy-in-Blood enters with a bleeding resident of the city holding his garment. He turns and declaims in Sanskrit.)

Blood : *The moment I handle a razor to shave, humans lose all hope of living.*
The moment I prepare to perform my functions as a barber, my heart gets anxious to see waves of blood flowing out of human bodies. (38)

Also,

Crying out in terrifying agony because their hands, feet and neck are tied, When I cut the nails of such humans, they certainly relinquish all hope of rebirth. (39)

(Looks at the assembly and hands over a mirror)

King : O Inclined-Vulva! You must accept this mirror first.

Vulva : (Takes it and looks at it)
O Great King! I am afflicted with an eye ailment called cataract. Hence, I am incapable of seeing the reflection of my face in the mirror in any way. Your Majesty must, therefore, receive the mirror.

King : O Ocean-of-Diseases! Despite your presence this procuress called Inclined-Vulva suffers from an eye ailment called cataract.

Diseases : Why don't you apply an iron rod heated in fire, held firmly and steadily in hands, on the pupils of the eyes. When no eyes remain, how can an eye ailment called cataract survive?

Streak : (Laughing) First the physician must apply the burning rod to his eyes and test the remedy himself?

Diseases : This prostitute mocks me, so it is pointless staying here.
(He leaves after that)

Buffoon : (Takes the mirror, looks into it and says with surprise)
Oh! Old-age has descended on me!

My hair have turned white, my teeth have decayed and are about to fall; the body too has become old and infirm, my eyes have cataract, the ears no longer hear any words, the flesh of the body too has become loose.
All these states of the body are due to old age; despite this state, my flirtatious heart constantly remains eager to embrace fair-complexioned whores: this act of the Almighty seems very strange to me. (40)

King : Listen barber! If you have to say anything on this subject, speak now.

Blood : O Mighty King! I have a quarrel with this person who is writhing in pain.

King : O Minister! Deliberate about dispensing justice to these two men.

Folly : O Barber! Tell me, who saw this blood billowing out first?

Blood : I saw it first.

Resident of the city : What do you mean when you say that you saw blood flowing out of my body first?

Folly : O Barber! How did you see it first?

Blood : (To himself) This praiseworthy minister is as eminent as the King! (In the Light) O Great King! I had pulled this person's fingers in order to clip his finger nails. That very moment this person covered his eyes with his fingers. Hence, my instrument went inside his eyes and broke. That is why he started bleeding.

Folly : He has said the right thing. O Resident! You better pay the barber the cost of the nail-clipping instrument.

Vulva : The Minister is as eminent as the King.

Door-Keeper : (Enters) O Great King! Mithyārṇava, Ocean-of-Deceit, a brahmin, wants to meet you.

Buffoon : Let him come in.

Door-Keeper : Come in (Having announced the presence of Ocean-of-Deceit, exits)

(Ocean-of-Deceit enters)

Deceit : O Great Preceptor! My son-in-law lives close to us. In his house, a brahmin has died. This brahmin studied the four Vedas, followed the rules of celibacy with distinction, bathed once a year and had many wounds caused by blows from the feet of flies. Troubled by the death of the brahmin, we started searching for a Pundit who knew the scriptures. We found you in the house of the Procuress. Now please tell us all the penances we need to undertake in order to atone for this sin.

Buffoon : (Pretends to think by tapping his finger on his nose, and after careful consideration, says) If the brahmin has really died, then his wife or son must be made to drink extremely hot water mixed with cow-dung. In this way, they too will attain a passage to heaven.

Deceit : (Says softly in the ear)

He did not die because of injuries caused by blows from the feet of flies. He died because he was lynched by the residents of the city for committing adultery with a washerwoman.

Buffoon : Then everyone has been freed from the taint of sin. The washerwoman contaminated with the sin of killing the brahmin should be ritually purified and brought back home.

Streak : Your erudition is praiseworthy.

Deceit : (Looks at Streak and speaks)

Who is that person who has gone to the shore of the Gangā and has worshipped Lord Śiva by offering lotuses?
Who is that person who has worshipped Lord Kāmadeva, the foe of Śambarā, with utmost attentiveness?
Also, who is that person, who gives up his life knowingly and selflessly when the Gangā meets the Ocean?
Similarly, who is that fortunate person in whose lap Streak, who fascinates the whole world, will sit and will adorn it even for a moment? (41)

Deceit : (Looks at everyone and speaks to himself)
I have come here to embrace a prostitute, but this place already has a considerable collection of villainous men.
There is little scope when leeches live on the body of leeches, that is why staying here is worthless.

King : Why hasn't the magistrate called Sādhuhiṁsaka, Tormentor-of-Righteous, not arrived yet?

(After this Tormentor, looking delighted, enters)

Tormentor : Sword-wielding thieves have created turmoil in the whole city. That is why, filled with happiness, I have come to meet a prostitute.

King : (Pretends to be concerned out of fear)
O Minister! Great fear has spread because of these thieves. What needs to be done in this regard?

Folly : O Great King! The army ought to be equipped properly. Once that is done, first and foremost I ought to be protected, then the Queen and then finally the palace ought to be made secure.

King : (Says painfully)
Sitting inside the palace, one gets to enjoy the glimpse of the moon;
Along with the Queen, I regularly keep awake all night because of fear of decayed walls falling.
One has to keep anti-snake venom at hand all the time as frogs croak all night long and there is fear of snakes coming to get them. That is why the Palace has to be secured first from the thieves. (42)

King : Oh! I wonder what is the Queen's condition currently.

Vulva : O Illustrious Minister! Tell me more about the Queen about whom the King looks so pained and concerned.

Folly : Doesn't a human require a thousand mouths like Ādi Śeṣa, the symbol of eternity, to describe the qualities of the Queen?

Vulva : Even then, tell me something. I want to hear of her virtues.

Folly : If you so request, then let me briefly describe her virtues to you—

Her face is dark like the moon on the night of the new moon,
She is as fair as collyrium, her lovely eyes are like that of a cat;
With a waist like a large pot and lofty breasts that hang below the navel—these qualities make the Queen an enchantress of the whole world. (43)

Vulva : O Friend! The King is foremost among the learned but you are the crest-jewel among all poets.

Folly : O Great King! If the threat of thieves has increased and spread widely, why not summon the Army Chief, Raṇajambuka, Jackal-of-War.

Jackal : (Jackal-of-War enters, turns and speaks with pride) – O Great King! Listen to the account of my valiant deeds.

King : Tell me.

Jackal : O Great King! Today I saw bee sucking nectar from a red flower.

King : And then?

Jackal : Soon after that, I donned a body armour, picked up my weapons and accompanied by four soldiers, I tied the bee with thick leather ropes and pulled it towards me.

King : (With delight) What next?

Jackal : After that the bee was hollowed out like a leather bag by my sharp sword.

King : There is no room for any doubt regarding your valour. You contain within yourself the strength of ten thousand elephants.

Folly : O Army Chief! The hour of war with the sinful has arrived. How enthusiastic are you about it?

Jackal : (Speaks in Sanskrit)

I faint and fall on the ground the very moment I see the red painted on my wife's feet while making love to her as I mistake it for blood; and I faint also when all parts of the earth are covered in the darkness of a new moon night.
Now, tell me what my condition would be if I had to see soldiers bathed in blood in the battlefield. (44)

Streak : (Laughs loudly)

Jackal : (In anger)
Oh! You wicked harlot! You ridicule me!! Why don't you engage in battle with me right away (makes a pretence of anger).

Door-keeper : O Great King! An astrologer named Mahāyātrik, Predictor-of-the-Great-Beyond, is at the door.

King : Let him come.
(The door-keeper speaks and exits)

Great-Beyond : (Enters, opens his scroll, turns towards the South, and reads)—

Let sun be located in your birth sign and destroy your position, let Jupiter be in your birth chart and increase your fears, let Saturn stay in your eighth house enhancing your pains and aches, let Mars also be in your eighth house and kill all members of your household and inflict weapons on you and then let the powerful Rāhu along with Sun be in your twelfth house and drain your wealth. Given the position of these powerful plants, the otherwise favourable effect of the moon, Venus and Mercury can hardly be favourable. (45)

Folly : You have heard the benediction. At this moment, the Great King wants to go to war. Therefore, find an auspicious moment for his 'great journey'.

Great-Beyond : The Great King's 'great journey' will be on Saturday morning, the day of the full moon, the lunar month of Śrāvaṇa, under the sign of Scorpio.

Tumour : Then he will surely die.

Great-Beyond : He will, then, carry away with him the demon of his subject's misfortunes.

Buffoon : (Looks east and west and speaks)—
The orb of the sun is about to sink and the orb of the moon is growing and about to rise.
The God of Love's angry eyes imitate the redness of the orbs of the sun and the moon because residents have been kept away from their wives. (46)

Buffoon : (Looks at Streak and says lovingly)
Tumour, my boy! It is evening. Hence, you go to Streak and whisper into her ear that I wish to spend the evening in meditation with her in a secluded spot.

Tumour : (Hears him and speaks to himself in Sanskrit)
This teacher of ours is wicked; he wishes to engage in amorous sport with this young woman.

Additionally,

Though I have diligently served my virtuous guru every day, what have I achieved doing it?
Though I have worshipped the sun every day, what have I gained out of it?
Though I have rigorously studied the Vedas, what benefit has it been to me?

Even if I were to attain heaven, how would I profit from it?
All these are fruitless if I cannot satiate the fire of love by perspiring after passionately embracing the urn-like lofty breasts of Streak. (47)

Tumour	:	It is useless to delay any further. Why don't I firmly embrace her and kiss her mouth. (Comes into the light and moves closer) O Streak! I want to speak to you.
Streak	:	If it is appropriate, then say it.
Tumour	:	(Speaks in Sanskrit):

The time of our youth is fleeting and remains only for ten to fifteen days; lofty and firm breasts sag and droop with age and cannot rise again.
O moon-faced Streak! There is no assurance how long life itself remains.
Knowing all this, when young women reject young men who come with the desire to make love, then the firm breasts of these young women manifest as thorns in the hearts of these youth. (48)

Streak	:	(Smiles a little)
Tumour	:	O Streak! I want to tell you a secret, so please hear me out. (He puts his mouth close to her ear and embraces her firmly, kissing her intensely on her mouth. (And, then, speaks in Sanskrit) *Even the Gods would not have drunk the nectar of Streak's lips. No wonder the Gods seem happily reconciled with nectar in the form of the moon that had fallen from Rāhu's mouth. (49)*
Buffoon	:	(With anger) You wicked boy! You will have to atone for having embraced and kissed Streak, who, I had desired all along.
Tumour	:	You must atone instead because you claim to desire a woman who has already been embraced by your disciple.
Buffoon	:	That organ of the body that gives the elephant's trunk its name, that organ of your body, namely, your hands should be chopped-off because you touched the girl desired by your preceptor.
Tumour	:	Since you are calling Streak, who was kissed by your disciple, as the woman you desire, the organ that adorns the loins of beautiful women is worth being chopped-off from your body.
Buffoon	:	Your teeth that are covered by your lips ought to be plucked out because you hurt Streak's lips with your teeth.

Tumour : Your lingam, penis, that word is formed by fastening a vowel ahead of the root 'ligi', that penis of yours is worthy of being uprooted. That is because with that penis you will harass the young lady who has been kissed by your disciple.

(In this way, both dance around quarrelling with each other and all bystanders laugh.)

(A bard speaks from the wings)

Closely pressed together, the bold and grown-up women's eyes are driven imagining the great exhilaration of the playful sex act.
The innocent and inexperienced women's indignant quivering eyes reflect dread at the thought of failing in the battle of pleasure.
The women whose men have been away on a voyage are teary-eyed, their hearts lonely—
Though not related by blood, all these women observe the impetuously violent orb of the sun setting behind the mountain with pain. (50)

Additionally,

With the setting of the sun-god in the West, the moon's rays now are scorching and shrivelling the lotuses.
The onset of the night has made the large black bees leave the lotuses, while the setting sun has deprived them of light——
They are like a woman distressed with worry thinking about her husband gone on a voyage. (51)

(A second bard sings)

Visible till a few moments back, where has the orb of the sun gone?
Where has the cry of the cakra bird, heard till a few moments ago, gone?
Having abandoned their bashfulness only a few moments back, where have the swans engaged in amorous play gone?
The moon has risen, an angry red reflecting the setting sun's rays, resembling an angry woman's face when she discovers that her husband is attached to someone else;
Hearing singing of the bees, the cluster of lotuses awaken and seem like laughing in order to show their happiness. (52)

Further,

Seeing the disc of the rising moon, a doubt enters the heart whether it really is the beautiful cup for dinking nectar for heaven's inhabitants?
Or is it the ball with which Rati, Kāmadeva's wife, plays?
Otherwise, is it a cluster of foam in the Gaṅgā?
Or, still further, is it King Kāmadeva's umbrella?
Or is it a vast treasure of glory? (53)

Folly : Since it is evening now, why don't you go to perform your daily rites?

King : What good will come of performing daily rites?
I am worried about the turmoil brought about by the thieves. Even then, I will go. But wait for a bit: watch the hostility between the preceptor and his disciple.

Buffoon : (With a staff in hand, he runs angrily)

Tumour : (Screams and shakes his entire body)

(After this both dance around quarrelling while each holds Streak's garment and says, 'She is mine'! 'She is mine'!)

Vulva : O Sir! O Lord! Please end this quarrel today.
It is night now. Tomorrow morning, a preceptor named Madanāndhamiśra, Blind-with-Passion, will be here to tutor Streak. You both will have to do whatever he commands.

Buffoon & Tumour : So be it.
(Everyone exits)

Sabhā-nirṇayo, Verdict of the Council, Act I of Hāsyārṇava Prahasanaṁ concludes.

Act II

(The next morning. Buffoon and Tumour enter)

Buffoon : (Looking towards the East)
Oh! The rays of the sun in the east look like the red vermillion adorning the parting on a woman's head.

(Turns and speaks while looking at the pond in front of him)

Having decked herself in anticipation of receiving her husband at night, the heroine finds him standing in front of her in the morning with the sun rising, having spent the night in amorous play with his mistress.
She looks at him angrily, with blood-shot eyes, resembling the red lotuses in the pond looking even more red in the morning red rays of the sun, the sun having spent the night in some other part of the earth. (1)

Further,

The flow of the morning breeze gives the heart great joy because the pleasant perfume of flowers is infused in it. It also bears the fragrance of the day-lotus, but also carries with it the sweet smell of deer-musk and vermillion, flowing red and black washed-off with the sweat produced by trembling women engaged in repeated amorous exertions. (2)

Buffoon and Tumour : (Both turn and come to Inclined-Vulva's house and enter. Together they say)
Where are Inclined-Vulva and Streak?

(Inclined-Vulva and Streak enter)

Buffoon : (Looks at Streak and speaks)

If Streak, whose face is like the autumnal moon, would look at me with a flirtatious glance, then who would even glance at the blue lotus, she, tender as the pleasing collyrium leaf that she is wearing in her ear? (3)

Additionally,

It is difficult even for Lord Śiva to resist Streak's eyes reeling with sleep but also the upright pupils of her flirtatious eyes giving side-glances. (4)

Tumour : O Inclined-Vulva! Has Madanāndhamiśra, Blind-with-Passion, not arrived yet?

(From the wings)

He whose sacred thread has become red from the fragrant unguents of prostitutes,
he whose eyes have become red from drinking excessive amounts of hemp liqueur,
he whose entire forehead is smeared with sandal-paste, and he who has given up performing religious worship—a man who embodies these virtues is himself arriving. (5)

(Blind-with-Passion is seen entering accompanied by Kulāla, Wild-Cock, a disciple).

Passion : (Looking ahead) Look!
On hearing the sound of bees encircling the mango trees and listening to the sweet singing sound of cranes and cuckoos, this springtime resounds with the warm sighs of beautiful women separated from their lovers.

Additionally,

The breeze from the south, having touched the cool water drops splashed by the hands of women playing in the waters of the Kaveri river, infused with the fragrance of white sandal, generating enthusiasm for amorous love, gently shaking the cluster of buds on mango trees, looks slightly scared by the touch of flowers in full-bloom on a vine, as if it had been in union with a menstruating woman. (6)

Passion : (To himself) How will I survive this spring season without a prostitute? (In the light) Wild-Cock, my child! Look, it is afternoon now—

Lord Surya is warming the earth with his rays. All the birds have entered the safety of the arbour created by the vine leaves. The flamingos have gone under a cluster of radiantly blooming lotuses and remain motionless. Tired and dispirited travellers, their hearts burning from the intense distress of long-standing separation from their wives, are sitting under the shade of branchless trees and writing something while constantly sounding out long sighs. (7)

Wild-Cock : O Good Sir! A procuress called Inclined-Vulva lives in this city. One hears that she is hospitable and serves guests well. That is why we will eat at her place.

Passion : Is she well-born?

Wild-Cock : Is there a doubt? Even an outcaste from the lowest caste does not drink water in her house.

Passion : (With enthusiasm) O child! Then, let's go.
(After this, both turn and go near Vulva's house before entering it)

Vulva : O Sir, Blind-With-Passion! Please sit on this beautiful seat.

Passion : (Pretends to sit, looks at everyone, and, then, speaks to himself) Isn't it a surprise that Streak, the jewel among heroines, is in front of me?

Streak's breasts, visible in the middle of her red dress, are the shape of a risen half-moon; they are like a radiant sliver of the moon rising from behind the eastern mountains.
She contracts her eyebrows, throwing passionate and flirtatious glances, causing the delusion of a bee pulling the petal of a large Ketaka flower.
Which man, watching this, does not get uneasy with longing and is not compelled to look at her. (8)

Additionally,

Streak's body is like a resplendent forest. Her lofty breasts look like impassable mountains, the region of her navel is low, her throbbing twitching arms enhance her beauty, the line of hair above her navel has the appearance of a beautiful cluster of bees.
Looking at all these states of Streak, one slightly fears that the God of Love himself has taken the form of a hunter, shooting sharp arrows in the form of flirtatious glances. Tell me, O my deer-like heart! In whose refuge will you go to protect yourself? (9)

Passion : (After this, he thinks to himself) How do I dupe Buffoon and Tumour? Perfect, I will cheat them by pretending to be a follower of the Vaiṣṇava faith. (In the light)

O Tongue! You must always repeat the name of Viṣṇu.
O Eye! God pervades the whole world—you must see in that fashion.
O Ear! You must always hear the glories of the Lord.
O Heart! You must understand with great certainty that Lord Nārāyaṇa alone is everyone's refuge. (10)

(Again, to himself) Ah! I have committed a great sin by invoking the name of the Lord. Now, what must I do to atone for this sin?

Buffoon : (Listens, and then says to himself) Blind-with-Passion is a crook, and he is trying to deceive by invoking Vaiṣṇava faith. Good, I will also show him something. (In the light)

He who is the crest-jewel of all the three worlds and whose appearance is like a sapphire, he, who like a bee, is after the lotus-like face of the goddess, Śrī Lakṣmī, he whose colour is like the smoke that induces tears in the eyes of the wives of demons—I always meditate upon Lord Kṛṣṇa in my heart. (11)

Passion : (Angrily) Wild-Cock, my child! You must now expand on the tenets of the Vaiṣṇava faith.

Wild-Cock : Sir! Whatever you command (Speaks in Sanskrit)

In Kaliyuga, the life-span of humans is expectedly short. On top of it, the wicked make other people fast and undertake various bodily mortifications, destroying the body as a result. Those blessed with wisdom realise the futility of bodily mortifications and relish a faith and a form of worship that includes savouring a life of licentiousness and the joys that prostitutes bring. (12)

Buffoon : (Angrily) Tumour, my child! You must expound the Vaiṣṇava faith.

Tumour : (Declaims in Sanskrit)

Even if one fasts despite great suffering for fear of social censure from foolish people, and even if one endures the inner pain caused by the apprehension of impending death at night, a human still needs to eat first thing in the morning in order to live.

This way, there is the real fear that remaining hungry and fasting would see life itself veritably end. How can one attain complete deliverance if such is the manner of death? (13)

Additionally,

One gains merit by observing painfully distressing forms of fasts—the faces of priests who say this ought to be smeared with ashes. Ultimate release is possible only when the supreme and incomparable Lord Śiva is propitiated with meat, fish and women. (14)

Passion : (Listens, and then, speaks to himself)

This preceptor is crafty, so it is not possible to deceive him. It is futile to ensnare an old cat by feeding him sour gruel. Good, I will cheat him by being modest. (In the light)

O Lord! I bow to you.

Buffoon : (Loudly) O Friend, may you live long!

But it does not seem proper for people like you to greet me first when Inclined-Vulva, the woman of the multitude, is here.

Passion : Oh! I mistook you for Inclined-Vulva and greeted you.

Buffoon : (Laughing) He is truly blind with passion. That is why he confuses a man for Inclined-Vulva, the procuress.

Passion : (Going close) O Inclined-Vulva! I offer my respectful greetings.

Vulva : O Daughter! Raise him and pronounce a blessing upon him.

Streak : (Standing up) May Gaurī, Lord Śiva's consort, be pleased with you.
(Streak says this and then pretends to be shy)

Passion : Oh! Looking at Streak surprises me -
Both of the fawn-eyed Streak's legs manage with great difficulty to bear the weight of her extremely large buttocks. How can her singular waist bear the weight of both her lofty breasts, breasts that resemble the cheeks of elephants. (15)

Vulva : Good Sir! Eminent Brahmin! I am informing you that today a fire-offering for the God of Love is being organised in our house.
Hence, please officiate over it and bring it to completion.

Passion : (To himself)
The hollow of the loins of the fawn-eyed Streak will function as the altar for the sacrifice; near her loins is her vagina, that spot coveted by pleasure-loving men, which will act as the fire pit; her breasts will work as the fruit meant for ritual offering. The excessively burning fire of amorous passion will act as the fire for the sacrifice; I will act as the officiating priest and my semen will be the material offered in the fire, while my penis will act as the wooden ladle, the sphya. Having in possession these material that produce instant gratification, which man will forego performing such an amorous fire sacrifice? (16)

(In the light) O Inclined-Vulva! Old age has made your body frail. That makes you incapable of performing your duties. You must, therefore, appoint your daughter to collect the material for the sacrifice.

Vulva : Daughter! Please follow the wishes of the venerable brahmin.
(Streak enters the house)

Tumour : (Approaches) First resolve the quarrel between us, preceptor and disciple.

Passion : Child! Wait a moment. By then, the ritual sacrifice will be over.

(Passion enters the house, and, after having intense sexual intercourse with Streak, speaks joyfully)

Her breasts have got crushed because of embraces, her face is bathed in perspiration due to extreme exertion; she closes her eyes and makes a sound to express thrill when kissed, she who is praised with flattering language by deceivers; her eyebrows are beautiful and her side-long glances also happen to be fickle—a whore of these qualities can be savoured by only those humans who accumulate various kinds of merits over a hundred years. (17)

Buffoon : (Looks at Streak and speaks to himself)

The collyrium in Streak's two beautiful eyes has been washed away, the red on her lips too has got washed out, the bun of hair on her head has loosened, the sweat caused by amorous exertions has wiped away the sandal paste from her body.

Her thighs no longer are quivering, her hands are suffused with weakness and her chest is repeatedly trembling.

Looking at these signs, it seems certain that she is coming this way after sexual intercourse. (18)

Wild-Cock : (Walks in front and laughs loudly) O Gentlemen! One person has completed the ritual sacrifice.

Passion : (Shuts his left eye to wink and stops him)

Wild-Cock : What would you achieve stopping me? One man's accumulated merit hardly purifies another man, does it?

Passion : O child! Wait for a minute.

Buffoon : (Smiling) O Great Blind-with-Passion! I have now learned about the completion of your sacrificial ritual. Despite that, you must dispense justice between the two of us. (In Passion's ear) You must act in a way that I may get married to Streak.

Passion : We both should get married to her.

Buffoon : What is the harm in that? Look—

In this world, King Bhoja's daughters, Kuntī and Madrī, were married to six kings, namely, Dharma, Pavan, Indra, the two Aśvinī Kumar twins, and Pāṇḍu, and were still called faithful wives. Draupadī too was the wife of Yudhiṣṭhira, Bhīma, Arjuna, Nakula and Sahadeva, the five Pāṇḍavas. This implies that a woman being married to many men is hardly a sin, is it? (19)

Wild-Cock : (To himself) These two wicked men have joined together. I too must now make friends with Tumour. (Turns and embraces Tumour and whispers to him in his ear)—

O Friend! Look, these two men have forged a friendship and they will both marry Streak.

So, why don't we both marry Inclined-Vulva instead?

Tumour : My friend! I don't think you have said the right thing. We have no experience of sexual intercourse with an old woman. Again, it is very sad that these two old men might marry Streak, a woman who can enchant all the three worlds. A jasmine garland does not grace the wrists of a monkey, foolish rustics do not have the discernment for deer-musk, and a pearl necklace does not beautify the breasts of a woman who has lost her youth.

Wild-Cock : My friend! How long do you think these two old men will live? After these two die, we both will marry Streak.

Tumour : This is right, but I still feel sad.

Wild-Cock : When these two old men go out every day to beg for alms, Streak will be staying at home when they are away. Inclined-Vulva's eyes are afflicted with cataract. So during this period we should be able to fulfil our cherished aim.

Tumour : O friend! Let what you say indeed happen.

Vulva : (Laughing to herself) Both these crooks have aligned, and now they are getting to know each other.

Passion : O distinguished teacher! What is the bone of contention between the two of you? What is the problem?

Buffoon : He wants to marry Streak, but I desire her.

Passion : O Tumour! What do you have to say about this problem?

Tumour : Even though I have embraced and kissed Streak, he still wants to marry her?

Passion : I know the essential nature of justice; there is little joy in relishing the shrivelled and the emaciated.
Your preceptor initially desired Streak, so in some part she belongs to him.
But after our settlement she is entirely mine.
(After saying this, whirls around) O child!
My child! You are a groom of twelve years.
Inclined-Vulva, who is more than a hundred years old, and who keeps count of paramours by counting the wrinkles on her body, is the right girl for you.

Wild-Cock : (Comes close and speaks in Sanskrit)
Since you have forged the settlement, and I am your disciple, Streak is also mine.

Passion : Tumour, my child! Say yes, and along with Wild-Cock, my disciple, agree to marry Inclined-Vulva.

Tumour : Whatever the Venerable Brahmin commands.

Vulva : (Inclined-Vulva speaks to herself in Sanskrit)
Oh! The creator seems pleased with me. I am getting two young husbands in my old age.

Buffoon : (Looks at Tumour, and, smiling, speaks to himself)—
What will this boy do with his little penis when inserted in a hole from which the body of a baby has emerged? (20)
(In the light) The time of the wedding is drawing close. Hence, why don't you summon Mahānindaka, Mighty-Censurer, who lives in the disputed Southern land.

(Mighty-Censurer enters and looks at everyone. Then, he speaks with great pride) –

Censurer : *Is there any brahmin in the entire cosmos capable of conducting doctrinal debates with me matching my erudition and family line? (21)*
(Again, with pride) I have composed the four Vedas.

Tumour : Sir! The Vedas emerged from the mouth of Lord Brahmā. How could you have composed them?

Censurer : (Angrily) Ah! You consider that silly Brahmā to be the composer of the Vedas! I had been to heaven to check Brahmā's family line. Listen—
When Lord Śaṅkara washed Brahmā's feet with water of the Gangā locked in his hair, an infuriated Brahmā struck Lord Śaṅkara with his hands and beat him. Driven by fear, Lord Śaṅkara paid Brahmā obeisance, but Brahmā did not bless Lord Śaṅkara with long life.
When the preceptor of the gods came in front of him, he showed contempt by not even looking at him, believing the preceptor of the gods to be a sinner for receiving gifts from the thirty-three gods. (22)

Passion : Desist from this torrent of words.
You must now complete these two weddings.

Censurer : I don't take things in the form of donations and gifts.

Wild-Cock : What is the harm in accepting gifts from a prostitute?

Censurer : You are right. Before this, I did not know that this procuress is of noble descent.
(With respect) O Lord! Which woman will marry which man?

Buffoon : *The fawn-eyed Streak will marry us, the two suitable preceptors, while Inclined-Vulva, whose eyes are afflicted with cataract, will marry these two disciples. (23)*

Censurer : (Laughing, to himself) Ah! This is surprising.
(Looks at Streak)
It is surprising that—
Even when wounded to the quick by the sharp arrows of her eyes, is there a man who, despite this injured state, denies desiring to be with the fawn-eyed Streak? (24)

Additionally,

Streak's extremely white eyes, with flirtatious pupils in the middle of these eyes, capable of tearing apart even a strong heart, resemble milk-like poison emerging from the churning of the ocean. Even Lord Śiva is not powerful enough to endure this. (25)
But at this moment if I do not firmly embrace Streak, I might not remain alive.
(In the light)
Despite the white radiance emanating from her moon-like face, the fawn-eyed Streak's covered breasts are not budding. But despite the presence of her moon-like face, her frowning lotus-like eyes are opening. This blossoming of her lotus-like eyes alone is repeatedly raising doubts in my heart. (26)

Also,
Oh! These people are foolish—
The fawn-eyed Streak's lips are nectar to be drunk, the place above her thighs are her mountain-like breasts where one ought to live, her deer-like eyes are the only friends, her beautiful sentences are like reciting an excellent mantra invocation, and her lotus-like body is worthy of meditating upon—If a grove for ascetics resembling her body is there, wonder why the learned sages go to the forest for religious austerities? (27)

Listen! Listen! Buffoon! Why don't you call the astrologer named Mahāyātrika, Predictor-of-the-Great-Beyond, to fix an auspicious moment for the wedding?

Great-Beyond : (Great-Beyond enters, opens the almanac and says) O Priest! What needs calculating?

Passion : Find an auspicious moment for the wedding.

Great-Beyond : (Placing his little finger on the ground)
Whatever be the auspicious moment, whatever the day of the week, whatever be the lunar asterism, the work that needs to be done should be done. (28)

Censurer : (To himself) This astrologer is competent.
(In the light) Listen astrologer! This kind of auspicious moment does not have a conjuncture of widowhood, does it?

Great-Beyond : Is the earth devoid of men for these women to be widowed forever?

Censurer : O Buffoon and all other people! Take Bilva, the leaf of the wood-apple tree, and garlands in your hands and go near your prospective brides.

Great-Beyond : These adornments are fit for men who are nearing their death.

(All the men take the hands of their brides and sit down: Inclined-Vulva between the two disciples and Streak between the two preceptors. With immense sadness, Streak says to herself)—

Streak : *I sat in extremely desolate places and worshipped the Goddess Pārvatī; every day, with my heart filled with utter devotion I had prayed to Kāmadeva, the God of Love. The prayers and devotion to all the gods like Pārvatī and Kāmadeva is bearing fruits today—my marriage to these two old brahmins is as frighteningly painful as a death sentence, one that will push me closer to death. (29)*

Censurer : O Paramour! Get the Madhuparka, a mixture of honey, milk, curd, sugar and ghee.

Paramour : (Speaks after coming close) Sir! There is no honey, but just milk and water.

Censurer : Bring.

Paramour : (Brings milk and water and gives it)

Censurer : (Looks at each groom)

You are humans that have been burnt by the fire of the cremation ground and have been abandoned by your friends and relatives.

You must bathe and drink this milk and feel happy drinking it. (30)

(Takes Durvā, panic grass, and rice in hand)

In this world, the death of creatures is inevitable and this life is like a dream—you must think this way about life and death and not lament about these events. (31)

(Gets up and speaks loudly) *You who rely on the Great Sleep, you who lie on the Great Bed of the funeral pyre—may you all reside in the cremation ground. (32)*

(Sprinkles panic grass and rice on everyone's head)

Great-Beyond : Sleeping on a pyre in a cremation ground for those who marry is only appropriate.

Censurer : (Coming close) Tumour! You must first offer me the fee for having accepted a girl who is a hundred years old.

Tumour : (Offers sweets made with powdered hemp)

Censurer : May you flourish! (Takes the sweets and touches them to his head reverentially with great joy)—Om! I bow to the Goddess Gāyatrī (throws a part of the sweets on the ground and speaks enthusiastically after eating the rest)—

They cause great joy in matters of amorous love, make one's speech like the rain of nectar and fill one's eyes with desire—victory to sweets made with hemp. (33)

Vulva : The Mighty-Censurer comes from an illustrious family-line.

Censurer : (Comes closer) O Eminent Brahmins, please offer me the fee for giving away the bride.

Buffoon and Passion : Wait for four years.

Censurer : Then for four years she will remain a harlot [Bandhakī].

(He holds Streak's hand and happily dances with her)

Great-Beyond : Mighty-Censurer! This is hardly expected of you at this juncture.

Censurer : (With joy)

I have got Streak, who is a joy to behold for all human-kind, released now from the clutches of a pack of wicked men; I have got her for myself. That is why my heart is filled with joy.

It is my great desire to retire to the pleasure-house and mark her with various kinds of weapons of gratification, waging a tremendous amorous battle with her. (34)

(The Prahasanaṁ named Hāsyārṇava ends)

5

हास्यार्णवप्रहसनम्

प्रथमोऽङ्कः

स्वेदस्यन्दितसान्द्रचन्दनचयं दोर्वल्लिबन्धश्रमात्
ऊर्ध्वश्वासपरिस्खलत्स्मरकथं सन्दष्टदन्तच्छदम् ।
शीत्काराञ्चितलोचनं सपुलकं भ्रान्तभ्रु नृत्यत्करं
पार्वत्यां सुरतं मुदे रसवतामास्तां मृडानीपतेः ।।1।।

अपि च –

स्वर्भानुः सुरवर्त्मनाऽनुसरति ग्रासाभिलाषादसा-
बिन्दोरिन्दुमुखि! ग्रसेत किमुत भ्रान्त्या भवत्या मुखम्? ।
इत्थं नाथगिरा नभोऽर्पितदृशो वक्त्रे भवान्या भृशं
मानिन्याः कृतचुम्बनस्त्रिनयनः स्तादिष्टसिद्ध्यै सताम् ।।2।।

[नान्द्यन्ते सूत्रधारः] । अलमतिविस्तरेण, यस्य –

हास्यप्रस्फुटदन्तमौक्तिकचयच्छायामनोज्ञानना
नानाऽलङ्कृतिसत्कृता रसवतां चितप्रमोदस्थली ।
स्वच्छन्दं वरवर्णिनी रसवती सीमन्तिनीव स्वयं
रम्या श्री-जगदीश्वरस्य कविता सच्चित्तमानन्दयेत् ।।3।।

(अस्ति च तस्य कवेर्निजकुलकमलप्रकाशकदिनकरस्य त्रिपुरहरचरणप्रणामचन्द्रमःप्रकाशितकवित्वकैरवस्य मां प्रति निदेशः, - "त्वमिह सुरभिसमयोचितेनास्मद्विरचितेन हास्यार्णवनाम्ना प्रहसनेन विदग्धसमुदायानां हृदयानन्दमुत्पादय" इति । अवश्यमेतत् शासनमनुष्ठेयम्, यतो विदग्धजनमण्डितायां संसदि रसवत्या वाचा विलसितुं नर्तितुञ्च ममापि चित्ते कौतूहलमस्ति, अतस्तत् सङ्गीतकमवतारयामि । (परिक्रम्यावलोक्य च) अहो! कुसुमसमयरमणीयता चेतो हरति । यतः-

चञ्चति चन्दनपवने ध्वनति च मधुमत्तमधुव्रते मधुरम् ।
कूजति कोकिलनिकरे न हरति सुरभिर्मनः कस्य? ।।4।।

अन्यच्च, -

उड्डीयते स्खलति गुञ्जति कुञ्जमध्ये
पुष्पाणि चुम्बति परिष्वजते द्विरेफीम् ।
घूर्णन् भ्रमत्यपि परागविधूसराङ्गो
भृङ्गोऽद्य किं न कुरुते मधुपानमत्तः? ।।5।।

तत् कथमत्र ललनां विना विनोदः ? (परिक्रम्य नेपथ्याभिमुखं पठति) –

भृङ्गारसक्तनलिनीदलसत्कटाक्षे!
पीयूषरश्मिवदने! मदनेषुतुल्ये! ।
कन्दर्पसर्पपरिदष्टसुधे ! विदग्धे !
स्निग्धे ! प्रिये ! त्वरितमागमनं विधेहि ।।6।।

(प्रविश्य नटी) । अज्जउत्त ! एसम्हि दे आस्माणियोअएण समाअदो, ता अणुग्गहबअणं पसादीकरीअदु । (आर्यपुत्र ! एषाऽस्मि ते आज्ञानियोगेन समागता, तस्मादनुग्रहवचनं प्रसादीकुरु ।)

सूत्र - आर्य्ये! पश्य –

आशासु प्रसरन्ति कोकिलकलस्वाना निकुञ्जान्तरे
गुञ्जन्तो भ्रमराः समुत्कमनसश्चुम्बन्ति पुष्पावलीम् ।
स्पर्शोत्साहरितमल्लिकापरिमलः श्रीखण्डवायुर्वह-
त्येवं कं न करोत्ययं स्मरशराक्रान्तं वसन्तोदयः ? ।।7।।

अन्यच्च –

हृष्टाऽन्यपुष्टमधुरध्वनिभिर्नवोढाम्
अध्यापयन्ति किल माधविका व्रतत्यः ।
आलिङ्ग्य चूतमसकृत् कलकण्ठशब्दं
नूत्नप्रसूनपुलकं कुसुमागमेऽस्मिन् ।।8।।

नटी – (किञ्चिदन्यचित्ततां नाटयति) ।

सूत्र – आर्य्ये ! किमिति अन्यचित्ताऽसि ? ।

नटी – ण सुणिदं अज्जउत्तेण ? । (न श्रुतम् आर्य्यपुत्रेण ?।)

सूत्र – किं तत् ? ।

नटी – अज्ज ! अज्जेब णियदांतउरबासिणा अणअसिंधुणा णरबइणा मंडलबिआरणा कादब्बा, तेण अस्मचित्तह्मि (आर्य्य ! अद्यैव नियतान्तःपुरवासिना अनयसिन्धुना नरपतिना मण्डलविचारणा कर्त्तव्या, तेनान्यचित्ताऽस्मि ।)

सूत्र – कान्ते ! किमेतत् सत्यम् ? ।

नटी – अध इं । (अथ किम् ।)

(नेपथ्ये)

घटयत घटजालं तोयशून्यं पुरस्तात्
पथि तुषनखलेखा क्षिप्यतां भो नियुक्ताः ! ।
निजपुरपरिचर्चां कर्त्तुमेवायमुत्को
नृपतिरनयसिन्धुस्तूर्णमागच्छतीह ।।9।।

सूत्र – (आकाशे कर्णं दत्त्वा आकर्ण्य च) –

नीतिर्भीतिमती दिगन्तमभजत् क्षिप्रं समं साधुभि-
र्धूर्त्तानां पटुतापरं परधनाकृष्टं न केषां मनः ? ।
कान्ता कस्य बलान्न केन रमिता राज्ये यदीयेऽधुना?
तस्य क्षौणिपतेः समागतिरिह स्थातुं न युक्तं प्रिये ! ।।10।।

तदितोऽन्यत्र गच्छावः (इति उक्त्वा निष्क्रान्तौ) ।

(इति प्रस्तावना) ।

(ततः प्रविशति सानुचरो नरपतिः अनयसिन्धुः ।

राजा – (स्वगतम्) अहो ! दुर्दैवं, कुसुमशरशरनिकरजर्जरशरीरेण रात्रिन्दिवं परवनितानिधुवनविलोनमनसा कियत्कालं पौरपरिचर्चा न कृता । (प्रकाशम्) । अये चरश्रेष्ठ ! अयथार्थवादिन् ! निरूप्यतां तावत् मण्डलम् ।

चरः - जं देओ आणबेदि । (यद्देव आज्ञापयति ।)

इति निष्क्रम्य समन्तादवलोक्य च पुनः प्रविश्य नृपकर्णसमीपे उच्चैः । देओ ! जाणिदं मंडलरहस्सं । (देव ! ज्ञातं मण्डलरहस्यम् ।)

राजा – कथय कथय ।

चरः – चिरआलं अविआलणाए मंडले सब्बो ज्जेब बबाहारो अलंगदो त्ति । (चिरकालम् अविचारणया मण्डले सर्व एव व्यवहारः अस्तं गतः इति ।)

राजा – (सक्रोधं) कुतः ?

चरः – (संस्कृतमाश्रित्य) देव !यतः, -

आलिङ्गन्ति निजाङ्गनां परवधूं हित्वा जनाः साम्प्रतं
नीचः सीव्यति सत्युपानहमहो ! सद्ब्राह्मणानां गणे ।
वन्दन्ते द्विजमन्त्यजे निवसति व्रीडाविहीना जना
एवं मण्डलवैपरीत्यमधिकं जातं महाभूपतेः ।।11।।

अपि च –

नारीणां नयनेऽञ्जनं न जघने सिन्दूरभामण्डिते
सीमन्ते न च नूपुरौ पदयुगे यावोऽपि नैवेक्षणे ।
वक्षोजे मणिमञ्जरी न चरणे काञ्ची कटौ नाधरे
चेत्थं वेशविपर्य्ययः प्रतिगृहं दृष्टः सकष्टं मया ।।12।।

राजा – (आकर्ण्य आत्मगतम्) । चिरकालविचारणया अयमव्यवहारो जातः पौराणाम् । भवतु, दण्डं विधास्यामि ।

(प्रकाशम्) । अये ! आहूयतां कुमतिवर्माख्यो मन्त्री ।

चरः - जं देओ आणबेदि । (यत् देव आज्ञापयति ।)

(इति निष्क्रम्य तेन सह पुनः प्रविष्टः) ।

(प्रविश्य कुमतिवर्मा वामपाणिना नृपतिं नमस्कृत्य) । अपृष्टोऽपि सन् प्रस्फुटम् आज्ञापयतु महाराज ! किम् अनुष्ठेयम् ? ।

राजा - मन्त्रिन् !अस्थानोचितस्थानं विना चिरं मण्डलचर्चा न क्रियते ।

मन्त्री – (ससम्भ्रमम्) । देव ! अत्रैव अस्ति परमरमणीयं स्थानम् ।

राजा – निवेदय निवेदय ।

मन्त्री – बन्धुरायाः कुट्टिन्याः प्राङ्गणम् ।

राजा – (साट्टहासम्) । कुमतिवर्मन् ! मम चित्तेन सममभिमन्त्र्य संसदि प्रविष्टवानसि, यतो देव्या गलितकुचस्पर्शविमुखस्य वाराङ्गनाऽऽलिङ्गनाय ममापि अभिलाषः, यतः उदरपतितस्तनीषु कुतः स्मरावस्थितिः ? ।

तथा च –

उत्तुङ्गस्तनशैलदुर्गविषमे वामेक्षणानां हृदि
स्थित्वा यत्र बलाद्भिनत्ति हृदयं यूनां सुतीक्ष्णैः शरैः ।
तस्मिन्मन्मथयुद्धमर्दनवशात् पातं प्रयाते स्तने
मन्ये दुर्गपराजयादपसरेद्भीरुः स पुष्पायुधः ।।13।।

मन्त्री – तदुपसर्पावः ।

राजा – (सोल्लासं मन्त्रिणा सह परिक्रामति)

चरः – (परिक्रम्य) । देअ ! एत्थ ज्जेब पूरदो घणदर घणसारसुरहिचंदणमिअणाभिबिबिहकुसुमपरिमलो ओसरदु, ता एदं बंधुराए मंदिरं तक्केमि, इदो अणुसरदु देओ । (देव ! अत्रैव पुरतो घनतरघनसारसुरभिचन्दनमृगनाभिविविधकुसुमपरिमलोऽपसरति, तस्मादिदं बन्धुराया मन्दिरमिति तर्कयामि, इतोऽनुसरतु देवः ।)

राजा – (प्राङ्गणमनुसृत्य सप्रमोदम्) । इदं बन्धुरायाः प्राङ्गणं, प्राप्तं मया तीर्थशतपर्य्यटनपुण्यम् ।

मन्त्री- क्व सा बन्धुरा कुट्टिनी ? ।

(ततः प्रविशति भुजङ्गशतपरिवेष्टिता बन्धुरा) ।

बन्धु - अहो ! अच्चरीअं !! अच्चरीअं !! णणु रे भुजंगा ! अणअसधुणरबइणो धूत्ताणां चक्कबट्टिणो समागमो बट्टदि, ता कधं तालजुअलझिल्लीमद्दणमिलिदाइं बसंतसमअमुद्दिसिअ गीदाइं गाइदु बिलंबीअद ? (अहो !

आश्चर्य्यम् !! आश्चर्य्यम् !! ननु रे भुजङ्गा । अनयसिन्धुनरपतेर्धूर्त्तानां चक्रवर्त्तिनः समागमो वर्त्तते, तत् कथं तालयुगलझिल्लीमर्दलमिलितानि वसन्तसमयमुद्दिश्य गीतानि गातुं विलम्बयत ? ।)

(उपसृत्य भुजङ्गाः । सहर्षम्) ।

महुमत्तमहुब्बदराअजुतो कलकंठविलासिणिगाणरुतो ।

जुअचित्तबिआरणपंचशरो तुह भोदु महुब्बहुप्पीदिअरो ।।14।।

(मधुमत्तमधुव्रतरागयुतः कलकण्ठविलासिनीगानरुतः ।

युवचित्तविदारणपञ्चशरः तव भवतु मधुर्बहुप्रीतिकरः ।।)

(इति पुनः पुनर्नाहयति) ।

राजा – (आकर्ण्य कर्णे स्वैरम्) । हे कुमतिवर्मन् ! किञ्चिदियं प्रार्थयते ।

कुमति – निखिले जगति महापातकिनो भवन्त एव, तत् सर्वान् विहाय ते शिरसि भविष्यति वज्रपातः ।

राजा – न ज्ञायते किमेवं भविष्यति, तदा किं विधेयम् ? ।

मन्त्री – दैन्यं प्रकटीकृत्य अत्रैव उपवासत्रयं विधेयमिति ।

राजा – (आत्मगतम्) । अलं भयेन, प्रणम्य एनां प्रतारयामि । (प्रकाशम्) । मातर्बन्धुरे । अयमहं प्रणमामि ।

बन्धुरा – (मिअंकलेहा दे सुप्पसम्मा भोदु ।) मृगाङ्कलेखा ते सुप्रसन्ना भवतु ।

राजा – (सहर्षमात्मगतम्) । निस्तीर्णोऽस्मि महापातकभयात्, न प्रार्थितभनया किञ्चित् । (प्रकाशम्) क्व सा मृगाङ्कलेखा ? ।

(ततः प्रविशति विशेषलङ्कृतशरीरलतिका मृगाङ्कलेखा) ।

मृगा - (सस्मितम्) । अंब ! को एषो ! । (अम्ब ! क एषः ? ।)

बन्धुरा – पुत्ति ! ण आणासि ? कणअसिंधु भुमिस्सरो दे दंशनत्थी ।

(पुत्रि! न जानासि ? अनयसिन्धुः भूमीश्वरः ते दर्शनार्थी ।)

मृगा – (सस्मितम्) । इदो अहिअं किं पुणं ? (इतोऽधिकं किं पुण्यम् ? ।)

राजा – (नायिकामवलोक्य) । अहो ! आश्चर्य्यमस्याः ।

सञ्जातेन्दुपराभवं परिलसद्यालोलनेत्राञ्जनं

भ्रान्तभ्रूलतमैणनाभितिलकं श्रीखण्डपत्रालकम् ।

बन्धूकाधरसुन्दरं सुरमुनिव्यामोहिवाक्यमृतं

त्रैलोक्याद्भुतपङ्कजं वरतनोरास्यं न कस्य प्रियम्? ।।15।।

अपि च –

अस्या धामसरोवरं भुजविसे वक्तारविन्दे भ्रम-

न्नेत्रभ्रू भ्रमरे सुयौवनजले कस्तूरिकापिङ्किले ।

वक्षोजप्रतिकुम्भिकुम्भदलनक्रोधादुपेत्य द्रुतं

मग्नश्चित्तमतङ्गजः कथमसावुत्थाय निर्यास्यति ? ।।16।।

(पुनर्बन्धुरामन्यमनस्कामवलोक्य) । बन्धुरे! कथमन्यहृदयाऽसि? ।

बन्धु - देओ ! मिअंकलेहां मम्महतंतं अज्झाबणत्थं बीस्मभंड उअज्झाओ आगमिस्सदि, एदेण अस्महिअआऽस्मि ।

(देव ! मृगाङ्कलेखां मन्मथतन्त्रमध्यापयितुं विश्वभण्डः उपाध्याय आगमिष्यति, एतेन अन्यहृदयाऽस्मि)

राजा – (सहर्षम्) । अस्माकं कुलपुरोहितः स एव ।

(नेपथ्ये)

दिनोपवासी तु निशाऽऽमिषाशी

जटाधरः सन् कुलटाऽभिलाषी ।

अयं कषायाम्बरचारुदण्डः

शठाग्रणीः सर्पति विश्वभण्डः ।।17।।

(ततः प्रविशति विश्वभण्डः कलहांकुरेण छात्रेण अनुगम्यमानः । परिक्रम्य समन्तादवलोक्य च) । अहो! अभिनवकुसुमकालो वर्त्तते ।

अपि च –

कुसुमशरसखो विनोदिबन्धु-
र्विविधविलासकलापमानधामा ।
मदयति हृदयान्ययं जनानां
सुरभिरिवासवसञ्चयः सुगन्धिः ।।18।।

(पुनः छात्रवलोक्य पठति)-

आकाशे प्रसरन्ति तालयुगलस्वानाः सझिल्लीरवाः
सर्वाशामुखरी ध्वनत्यविरतं मन्दं मृदङ्गध्वनिः ।
कर्पूरागुरुगन्धबन्धुरनिलो व्याप्नोति सर्वा दिशो
गेहे कस्य महोत्सवोऽद्य नियतं वत्स ! द्रुतं ज्ञायताम् ।।19।।

(परिक्रम्य कलहांकुरः) । भअबं ! बंधुराए कुट्टिणीए णिलए महुस्सबो बट्टदि । (भगवन्! बन्धुरायाः कुट्टिन्याः निलये महोत्सवो वर्त्तते ।)

विश्व – (सहर्षम्) । वत्स ! पूर्वसंवत्सरे भोजयितुं तया निमन्त्रिता वयं, तदयमवसरः ।

(इति परिक्रम्य बन्धुरायाः प्राङ्गणं प्रविष्टः) ।

बन्धु-उअज्झाअ! एदं भग्गासणं, उबबिसदु अज्जो । (उपाध्याय ! इदं भग्नासनम्, उपविशतु आर्यः ।)

विश्व – (नाट्येन उपविश्य ससम्भ्रमम्) । मातर्बन्धुरे ! प्रणमाणि ।

बन्धु-पुत्त !मअणसमुद्दसंतरणं भोदु । (पुत्र ! मदनसमुद्रसन्तरणं भवतु ।)

विश्व - (नायिकामवलोक्य) –

मदनपयोनिधितरणं भवति तदा पीवरकुचकुम्भो मे ।
यद्यवलम्बितुमस्या लभ्यत एवैणनेत्रायाः ।।20।।

नायिका – (सस्मितमालोकयति) ।

राजा – (स्वगतम्) । महामहोपाध्यायो विश्वभण्डः । कुलटाकुलार्चिताया बन्धुराया लब्धाशीर्वादः पार्श्वतः समुपविष्टः शुभाशीर्वादं सङ्ग्रहीतुम् । (प्रकाशम्) । भगवन् ! प्रणमामि ।

विश्व – भो कलहाङ्कुर ! द्रुतं देहि राज्ञे आशीर्वादम् ।

कुलहांकुरः – (साट्टहासं शक्राशनमृक्षितं दूर्वाऽक्षतमादाय संस्कृतमाश्रित्य उच्चैः) । नेत्रे पुष्पोदयो भवतु भवताम् ।

अपि च –

शत्रोर्वृद्धिर्भियो वृद्धिर्वृद्धिर्व्याधेर्ऋणैनसाम् ।
दुर्गतेर्दुर्मतेर्वृद्धिः सन्तु ते सप्त वृद्धयः ।।21।।

(इति पठित्वा राजशिरसि दूर्वाक्षतमर्पयति) ।

राजा – भगवन् ! कोऽयं दुष्टबटुः ?

विश्व – अयमविदितो भवता ?

निजवंशधूमकेतुर्भृशमघसेतुः प्रमादचयहेतुः ।
परवित्तहरणशूरः कुमतिः कलहाङ्कुरः क्रूरः ।।22।।

(पुनर्बन्धुरामवलोक्य) । भो वत्स ! कलहांकुर !–

प्रलम्बितपयोधरा क्षतरजा विकारास्पदं
सदा विगतहंसका तिमिरलुप्ततारारुचिः ।
तिरस्कृतनिशाकरा गतवया इयं बन्धुरा
सदा सपदि दृश्यतां जलधरागमश्रीरिव ।।23।।

वत्स ! वन्दनीयतरां बन्धुरामुपसृत्य नमस्कुरु ।

कलहा - (सहर्षोल्लासं परिक्रम्य बन्धुरायाश्चरणद्वयमध्यभागतो दण्डवत्प्रणम्य पुनरूर्ध्वजघनमालोक्य सहस्ततालमुच्चैर्विहस्य संस्कृतमाश्रित्य) । भो महामहोपाध्याय ! आश्चर्यमस्या बन्धुराया अधोमुखे श्मश्रुश्रेणी ।

अपि च –

स्तनौ तुङ्गौ निपतितौ कामसंग्राममर्दितौ ।
पुरस्तादवलोक्यास्या भगं शुष्कं भयादिव ।।24।।

बन्धु – (सस्मितम्) । णट्टो बटुओ, सत्थकं खलहांकुराहिधाणो इमस्स । (नष्टो बटुः, सार्थकं कलहांकुराभिधानमस्य ।)

विश्व – (नायिकामवलोक्य) । अहो । तरुण्या भावप्रकर्षः ।

स्वैरं सस्मितमीक्षते क्षणमलं व्याजृम्भटे वेपते
रोमाञ्चं तनुते मुहुस्तनतटे व्यालम्बते नाम्बरम् ।
आलिङ्गत्यपरां तनोति चिकुरं प्रत्युत्तरं याचते
केयं कामकलाविलासवसतिर्लोलेक्षणा भाविनी? ।।25।।

अपि च –

खेलत्खञ्जननेत्रया परिलसत्स्वर्णारविन्दास्यया
पीनोत्तुङ्गनिरन्तरस्तनभरव्यालोलसन्मध्यया ।
स्फीतस्फीतनितम्बया क्षणमपि व्यालोकितश्चानया
किं न स्याद्वशिनां वरः स्मरहरः स्मारैः शरैर्जर्जरः ? ।।26।।

बन्धु – उअज्झाअ ! एषा मिअंकलेहा मे पुत्ती मम्महतंतं पठिदुं सुसज्जिदा बट्टदि । (उपाध्याय ! एषा मृगाङ्कलेखा मे पुत्री मन्मथतन्त्रं पठितुं सुसज्जिता वर्त्तते ।)

विश्व – (विहस्य) । अस्माकमध्यापनशून्यं मन्दिरम् एव वर्त्तते ।

मृगा - अंब ! एसो बुड्ढसादुलो बिअ गलिदणखदसणो जआजीणपंजरो अदिहदब्बीड़ो अहणिसं मं बिडं बेदि । (मातः! एष वृद्धशार्दूल इव गलितनखदशनः जराजीर्णपञ्जरोऽतिहतव्रीडोऽहर्निशं मां विडम्बयति ।)

कलहा - (सक्रोधम्) आः पामरि! गणिए! परपुत्तबित्तहारिणि! अम्हाणं उअज्झाअं दिट्टा ण कुरु कुब्बबसइणं, जस्स णिहुअणअणुरत्ता बम्हणी णत्तंदिबं बिअड्ढाणां ठाणे बंधणिबहं सिक्खअंती अज्जबि भमइ अइसिणेहेण उअज्झाअपुरदो बैहब्बमंडणं कदुअ णिच्चं अणुमरणत्थं सुसज्जिदा भोदि तं बुड्ढं जप्पेसि? अबिअ, अज्जबि उअज्झाओ लज्जाउलो बसणं पलिहलिअ जणणंके सअणं कुणइ, एणं हदब्बीडं जप्पेसि ? । (आः पामरि! गणिके! परपुत्रवित्ताहारिणि! अस्माकम् उपाध्यायं दृष्ट्वा न कुरु कुव्यवसायिनं, यस्य निधुवनानुरक्ता ब्राह्मणी नक्तन्दिवं विदग्धानां स्थाने बन्धनिवहं शिक्षमाणा अद्यापि भ्रमति अतिस्नेहेन उपाध्यायपुरतः वैधव्यमण्डनं कृत्वा नित्यमनुमरणार्थं सुसज्जिता भवति तं वृद्धं जल्पसि? अपि च अद्यापि उपाध्यायः लज्जाकुलः वसनं परिहृत्य जनन्यङ्के शयनं करोति, एनं हतव्रीडं जल्पसि? ।)

(इति क्रोधं नाटयति)

मृगा – (विहस्य) । धणा सा बह्मणी, सिस्सो बि धणो तहा उअज्झाओ । (धन्या सा ब्राह्मणी, शिष्योऽपि धन्यः, तथा उपाध्यायः ।)

बन्धुरा - पुत्ति! एदं भणिदब्बं मंददमं, उअज्झाअं ण आणासि, बुड्ढोबि मअणकमलप्पआसो दिणणाहो अज्ज बीसभंडो धुत्ताणां उअज्झाओ । (पुत्रि! इदं न भणितव्यं मन्दतमम्, उपाध्यायं न जानासि, वृद्धोऽपि मदनकमलप्रकाशो दिननाथ आर्य्यः विश्वभण्डः धूर्तानामुपाध्यायः ।)

विश्व – (आकर्ण्य आत्मगतम् ।) अहो! आश्चर्यम् ।

प्राप्ता प्रस्फुटकाशपुष्पपदवी केशैस्तथैव भ्रुवा
सम्यग् लोचनपक्ष्मणा च जरसा जीर्णा च दन्तावली ।
शुष्कं मन्मथमन्दिरं निपतितौ शुष्कातिशुष्कौ स्तनौ
एतस्याः सुतरां तथाऽपि वचने जागर्त्ति पुष्पायुधः ।।27।।

भवतु एषाऽपि क्व यास्यति ? । (प्रकाशम्) । बन्धुरे! जरातुरा वेपमाना दृश्यसे ।

बन्धुरा - सच्चं, पूब्बअणुरत्तसिणेहाणं बिअड्ढाणां गुणं सुस्मरंती अणंगज्वराउला क्खु अहं (सत्यं, पूर्वानुरक्तस्नेहानां विदग्धानां गुणं सुस्मरन्ती अनङ्गज्वराकुला खलु अहम् ।)

विश्व – (विहस्य) । भो महाराज! मदनज्वरातुरा बन्धुरा ।

राजा – तत् कथं न आहूयते आतुरान्तकसुतो महावैद्यो व्याधिसिन्धुः ?

विश्व - अपि न ज्ञायते आतुरान्तकसुतोऽसौ ? किञ्च अस्य गुणा न ज्ञायन्ते ?

राजा – भवताऽपि न विदितं उपचारवचनम्?

नेत्रे तप्ता शलाका जठरगुरुगदे श्लीपदे छित्तिरङ्घ्रे-
रश्मर्यां नासिकायां वडिशमतिशितं तप्ततैलञ्च शूले ।
हृद्रोगे यन्त्रदारुद्वयनिबिडतरं बन्धनं मुष्कदेशे-
ऽप्येतैः रम्योपचारैर्नयति पितृवनं रोगिणं कं न चाशु ? ।।28।।

अपि च –

कासे धूमस्तुषाणां बलवति मरुति स्वेदभेदोपवासा
वन्हेर्मान्द्ये च पिष्टं सपिशितमनिशं वारिपानं कफार्त्तौ ।
पित्तार्त्तावारनालं त्रिकटुरपि जलद्रोणिका सन्निपाते
किं ब्रूमो व्याधिसिन्धोर्गुणमिह सुतरामेकवक्त्रेण सम्यक्? ।।29।।

(नेपथ्ये)

पानीयस्थूलपादे कथमपि धरया धारिते साङ्कुरौघे
हस्तन्यस्ताञ्चलाग्रप्रचलितपवनैर्वारयन् मक्षिकालीम् ।
कासात् कण्ठस्वनोघैः सपदि मुखरयन् दिङ्मुखं व्योमवीथी-
मप्येष व्याधिसिन्धुः प्रविशति सरुजामन्तको राजवैद्यः ।।30।।

(व्याधिसिन्धुः प्रविश्य शनैः परिक्रम्य सगर्वम्) ।

वैद्योऽहं व्याधिवर्गाणामाश्रयोऽप्ययशोनिधिः ।
मया चिकित्सितः सद्यो मार्कण्डेयो न जीवति ।।31।।

अपि च –

सर्वौषधानि तिष्ठन्तु चिकित्साऽपि च तिष्ठतु ।
मम दर्शनतो रोगी किल प्राणैर्विमुच्यते ।।32।।

व्याधि - (उपसृत्य) । भो भो महामहोपाध्याय! अयमहं नमस्करोमि ।

विश्व - कलहांकुर! देहि भिषजे शुभाशीर्वादम् ।

कलहा – (हस्तमुद्यम्य उच्चैः)

स्वल्पायुर्भव साम्प्रतं चिररिपुर्मा जीव दण्डद्वयं
वक्षस्ते खरकण्टको निविशतां भोगी गले चुम्बतु ।
अन्येषामपराधतस्तव शिरो राज्ञा च संयम्यतां
हा-भक्तो भव सर्वदा तव गृहे वह्निः सदा नृत्यतु ।।33।।

ध्याधि – अरे पामर बटो! मामवक्षिपसि ?

विश्व – (विहस्य) । भो व्याधिसिन्धो! तव पितुः आतुरान्तकस्य अन्तकालप्राप्तस्य कुशलम् ?

व्याधि – कुतः कुशलं भवद्दर्शनं विना ? (नायिकामवलोक्य) ।

कस्य न लुब्धं हृदयं काञ्चनरुचिना कुचद्वयेनास्याः ।
आलोक्य हेमकुम्भौ न भवति भुवि कस्य वा लोभः ? ।।34।।

विश्व- भो महावैद्य! कञ्चित् चिकित्साप्रश्नो मां मुखरयति ।

व्याधि – (सगर्वम्)

पिण्डाय तण्डुलतिलप्रचयं निधाय
पाणौ खनित्रमपि चारुचितार्थमेव ।
वैद्योऽस्मि रोगिजनबान्धवसम्प्रदायैः
प्रष्टव्य एव हृदयेषु विमुच्य मोहान् ।।35।।

विश्व - (विहस्य) । महावैद्योऽसि । (पुनः सहर्षम्) महावैद्य! प्रचुरतश्रृङ्गाररसप्रागल्भ्यात् श्लेष्मातुरा बन्धुरा, तत् क्रियतामस्या
उपचारः ।

व्याधि – सुतप्तकटुतैलेन कथमस्या गुदे नस्यं न दीयते ? तत् अलं
विलम्बेन ।

बन्धु - (विहस्य आत्मगतम्) । एसो बुद्धिरहिदो बेज्जो (प्रकाशम्) । भअबं! भग्गेण पुच्छिदब्बो महाबेज्जो । (एष बुद्धिरहितो वैद्यः भगवन्! भाग्येन प्रष्टव्यो महावैद्यः ।)

विश्व - (आकाशमवलोक्य) । आः! सहस्रावधानेन मया विस्मृतः प्रश्नः । (बिहस्य) । वत्स कलहांकुर! स्मारय वैद्यप्रशनम् ।

कलहा - (प्रस्फुटम्) । महाबेज्ज! मिअकलेहाए पउरचंदणकुंकुमकत्थुरिआपरिलेबणेण गात्तकंडुअणं समुपपणं, ता एत्थ किं कादब्बं ता भण । (महावैद्य! मृगाङ्कलेखाया प्रचुरचन्दनकुङ्कुमकस्तूरिकापरिलेपनेन गात्रकण्डूयनं समुत्पन्नं, तदत्र किं कर्त्तव्यं तत् भण ।)

बन्धु – (स्मितं कृत्वा आत्मगतम्) । जधा उअज्झाओ सिस्सोऽबितधा, जुत्तं भस्सपुंजे सारमेआबट्ठाणम् । (यथा उपाध्यायः शिष्योऽपि तथा, युक्तं भस्मपुंजे सारमेयावस्थानम्) ।

व्याधि –

वारिपर्णीचयैः साकं घृष्ट्वा वृश्चिकमङ्गतः ।

दातव्यो वानरीरेणुः सद्यः कण्डूहरो हि सः ।।36।।

बन्धु - सुट्ठु ओसहं (सुष्ठु औषधम्) ।

विश्व - भो शिष्य! भवताऽपि विस्मृतम् ।

कलहा - (स्मृतिमभिनीय) । हुं स्मरिदं । महाबेज्ज! सुरदसमरबिमद्दणादो मुंडपीडातुरा बंधुरा, ता एत्थ ज्जेब किं करीअदु? (हुं स्मृतम् । महावैद्य! सुरतसमरविमर्दनात् मुण्डपीडातुरा बन्धुरा, तदत्र किं करोतु?)

बन्धु - (सस्मितं स्वयमुपसृत्य) महाबेज्ज! जाणिदं दे बिज्जत्तणं, तहाबि कहणिग्गहत्थं ओसहं भण । (महावैद्य! ज्ञातं ते विद्वत्त्वं, तथाऽपि कफनिग्रहार्थम् औषधं भण) ।

व्याधि - (क्षणं विचिन्त्य) । ही! ही! कथमेव न निगद्यते? पुरा राज्ञो मरुत्प्रागल्भ्यात् सिंहासने उपविष्टस्य श्लेष्मा जातः, तदा अस्मत्पित्रा चरकसुश्रुतवाग्भटनागार्जुनतत्त्वविदा आतुरान्तकेन नृपतेर्लोचनद्वयं क्षारचूर्णेन निर्मार्ज्य जलौकाशतं प्रदाय श्लेष्मा अपक्षयितः ।

बन्धु-एत्थ ज्जेब किं कादब्बम् ? (अत्रैव किं कर्त्तव्यम्?)।

व्याधि - अल्पोपचारसाध्ये अलं गुरूपचारेण ।

वरटो भृङ्गरोलश्च जलौका वाऽथ वृश्चिकः ।

घ्राणे नेत्रे च दातव्याः सद्यः श्लेष्मविनाशिनः ।।37।।

बन्धु – (विहस्य) । सच्चं आदुरांतकपुत्तो तुमम् । (सत्यम् आतुरान्तकपुत्रस्त्वम् ।)

(नेपथ्ये कलकलः)

राजा – (आकाशे कणं दत्त्वा आकर्ण्य च प्रकाशम्) । अये! प्रतीहार! ज्ञायतामेतत् को मम दर्शनार्थी, तं प्रवेशय ।

प्रविश्य प्रती-जं देओ आणबेदि (निष्क्रम्य सम्यगवलोक्य पुनः प्रविष्टः) । देअ!रत्तकल्लोलणामहेओ णाबिदो एक्केण पोरजणेण रक्तकलेबरेण अंचलगहीदो बट्टदि । (यत् देव आज्ञापयति । देव! रक्तकल्लोलनामधेयो नापित एकेन पौरजनेन रक्तकलेवरेण अञ्चलगृहीतो वर्त्तते ।)

राजा – प्रवेशय ।

प्रती – (निष्क्रम्य पुनः प्रविश्य च तथा कृत्वा) । देअ! एस रत्तकल्लोलो णाबिदो । (देव! एष रक्तकल्लोलः नापितः ।)

(इति निष्क्रान्तः)

(ततः प्रविशति रक्तलिप्ताङ्गेन पौरजनेन अञ्चलगृहीतो रक्तकल्लोलः, परिक्रम्य संस्कृतमाश्रित्य पठति) ।

मयि क्षुरं गृह्णातिमानुषाणां भवेक्षणाशा तनुतामुपैति ।

स्ववृत्तिनिर्वाहपरे च रक्तचयोर्मिमालाऽऽकुलिता तनुः स्यात् ।।38।।

अपि च –

आर्त्तनादमधिकं प्रकुर्वतां हस्तपादगलबन्धपीडनात् ।

यं छिनद्मि नखरं नृणामहं स प्ररोहति पुनर्न जन्मना ।।39।।

(सभास्थानमवलोक्य दर्पणमर्पयति) ।

राजा - बन्धुरे! आदौ मुकुरं गृह्णातु भवती ।

बन्धु – (गृहीत्वा अवलोक्य च) । भअबं! तिमिराउला म्हि, दप्पणे ण कधंपि मुहाकिदिं पेच्छम्हि, ता दप्पणं गेह्णदु अज्जो । (भगवन्! तिमिराकुलाऽस्मि, दर्पणे न कथमपि मुखाकृतिं प्रेक्षिष्ये, तद्दर्पणं गृह्णातु आर्यः ।)

राजा – भो व्याधिसिन्धो! भवदधिष्ठानेन तिमिराकुला कुट्टिनी?

व्याधि-कथम् अग्निवर्णशलाका स्थिरहस्तेन अस्या लोचनतारकामध्ये न दीयते? तर्हि चक्षुषोरभावात् कुतस्तिमिरता?

मृगा - (विहस्य) । पढमदो बेज्जस्तु लोअणे परीक्खीअदु । (प्रथमतः वैद्यस्तु नयने परीक्षते।)

व्याधि- अलमिहावस्थानेन, गणिकाऽपि माम् उपहसति ।

(इति निष्क्रान्तः)

विश्व - (मुकुरं गृहीत्वा अवलोक्य च ससम्भ्रमम्) । अहो! वार्धक्यं जातम्!!

शुक्लत्वं जरसा कचेषु दशनाः शीर्णा विशीर्णा तनु-
स्तैमिर्यं नयने श्रुतौ न च वचोलब्धिः श्लथत्वं पले ।
अस्माकन्तु कथं तथाऽपि विलसद्वारङ्गनाऽऽलिङ्गन-
व्यामोहाय मनः सदैव बलते चित्रं चरित्रं विधेः ।।40।।

राजा – अरे नापित! ब्रूहि स्वाभिमतम् ।

रक्त - देअ! एदेण दाब पीडाकादरेण समं अम्हाणं कलहो बट्टदि ।

(देव! एतेन तावत् पीडाकातरेण सममस्माकं कलहो वर्तते ।)

राजा - मन्त्रिन्! विचार्यतामनयोर्न्यायः ।

मन्त्री – अरे नापित! निगद्यतां प्रथमतः कस्य गोचरः?

रक्त – पढमं अम्हाणं । (प्रथममस्माकम्)

पौर – ममाङ्गे शोणितप्रवाहः प्रथमतो गोचरस्तव?

मन्त्री – अरे नापित! कथं ते गोचरः?

रक्त - (आत्मगतम्) । धणो मंतिअरो णरराअजोग्गो । (प्रकाशम्) ! मअबं! एदमज्जेणअरजणस्स णहरमूलाकस्सणात्थं लोअणमज्झिणिहिदं बडिसं भग्ग, एदेण कारणेण । (धन्यः मन्त्रिवरः नरराजयोग्यः । भगवन्! एतस्यैव नगरजनस्य नखरमूलाकर्षणार्थं लोचनमध्यनिहितं वडिशं भग्नम्, एतेन कारणेन ।)

मन्त्री – भद्रम् उक्तम् अनेन । अरे पौर! बडिशमूल्यं दातुमर्हसि ।

बन्धु – (सस्मितम्) । धण्ण मंतिअरो णरबइजोग्गो । (धन्यो मन्त्रिवरो नरपतियोग्यः ।)

(प्रविश्य प्रतीहारः)- भअबं! मिथाणबणामहेयो बम्हणो अज्जं
पेक्खिदुमिक्छदि। (भगवन्! मिथ्यार्णवनामधेयो ब्राह्मण आर्य
प्रेक्षितुमिच्छति ।)

विश्व-प्रवेशय ।

प्रती - (तथा कृत्वा निष्क्रान्तः) ।

(ततः प्रविशति मिथ्यार्णवः)

मिथ्या - (समन्तादवलोक्य) । भो महामहोपाध्याय! अस्मत्प्रतिवासिजामातृप्राङ्गणे कश्चित् ब्राह्मणश्चतुर्वेदाध्यायी ब्रह्मचर्यनिपुणः संवत्सरस्नायी मक्षिकापादाहतिव्रणितदेहो मृतः, तेन ब्रह्मवधेन व्याकुलीभूता वयमितस्ततो वेश्याप्राङ्गणे स्मार्त्तपण्डितमन्विष्यन्तो भवदन्तिकमागताः स्म, तदत्र कानि प्रायश्चित्तानि?

विश्व-(स्मृतिमभिनीय स्वनासापुटेऽङ्गुलं प्रदाय परमार्थतो निरूप्य
आह) । यदि स्वरूपं ब्राह्मणो मृतस्तदा तद्वनितायाः तत्सुतस्य वा मुखे गोमयजलं वह्निवर्णं कृत्वा प्रदीयतां; तेन उभयोर्दिव्या गतिः ।

मिथ्या - (कर्णे स्वैरम्) । मक्षिकापादाघातेन न मृतः, किन्तु रजक्यां रममाणः सर्वैः पौरजनैर्लोष्ट्रपातैर्हतः ।

विश्व-तदा सर्वे निस्तीर्णाः, निर्मज्जनं कृत्वा नीयतां तेन पापेन रजकी विलिप्ता ।

मृगा - धणं पंडिदत्तम् । (धन्यं पण्डितत्वम्) ।

मिथ्या – (नायिकामवलोक्य) –

केनाराधि सरोरुहैः सुरनदीतीरे मृडानीश्वरः?
केनकारि च शम्बरारिचरणे भक्तिर्नितान्तं सदा? ।
केनाङ्गं सुरसिन्धुसिन्धुमिलने व्यामोचि निर्मोहतः?
यस्यैषाऽङ्कमलङ्करिष्यति जगद्व्यामोहिमूर्त्तिः क्षणम् ।।41।।

(पुनः सर्वानवलोक्य आत्मगतम्) । वाराङ्गनाऽऽलिङ्गनाय मम समागमः, किञ्चात्रैव धूर्त्तानां मेलकं, न हि जलौकसाम् अङ्गे जलौकानां गतिः, तदलमिहावस्थानेन । (इति निष्क्रान्तः) ।

राजा – अधुनाऽपि कथं नायातः साधुहिंसको दण्डपालः?

(ततः प्रविश्य साधुहिंसकः किञ्चित् मुदमभिनीय) । असिहत्तमोषएहिं ज्जेब सअलं णअरं ब्याउलीभूदं, हग्गे परमाणंदिदो गणिआसंदंसणत्थं आअदो

म्हि । (असिहस्तमोषकैरेव सकलं नगरं व्याकुलीभूतम्, अहं परमानन्दितः गणिकासन्दर्शनार्थम् आगतोऽस्मि ।)

राजा - (सभयं चिन्तामभिनीय) । मन्त्रिन्! चौरेभ्यो महती भीतिः, किमिदानीं करणीयम् ?

मन्त्री - देव! सैन्यं सुसज्जीकृत्य प्रथमतो मम रक्षणं विधेयं, ततो देव्यास्ततः प्रासादस्य च ।

राजा – (सकष्टम्) –

रात्रौ तारकनायकेक्षणसुखान्यूर्ध्वं पिधानं विना
नित्यं जर्जरभित्तिपातभयतो देव्या समं जागरः ।
यस्मिन् भेकरवागतोरगभयात् पाणौ सदैवौषधं
प्रासादः खलु तादृशः प्रथमतः संरक्ष्यतां चौरतः ।।42।।

हन्त! न जाने देव्याः कीदृशी गतिर्भविष्यति ।

बन्धु – अज्ज मंतिअर! किरिसी सा देई जं चिंतअन् देओ विसीददि? (आर्य! मन्त्रिवर! कीदृशी सा देवी यां चिन्तयन् देवः विषीदति?)

मन्त्री – तद्गुणवर्णने अनन्त इव कः सहस्रमुखः?

दर्शेन्दुतुल्यवदनाऽञ्जनपुञ्जगौरी
मार्जारचारुनयनाघटपीनमध्या ।
प्रोत्तुङ्गपीनकुचचुम्बितनाभिदेशा
त्रैलोक्यमोहवसतिः खलु कामिनी सा ।।43।।

बन्धु - भद्द! महीबालो बिअड्ढाणां अग्गगस्सो अबिअ तुमंक इचूडामणी (भद्र! महीपालः विदग्धानाम् अग्रगण्यः, अपि च त्वं कविचूडामणिः ।)

मन्त्री - देव! चौरभीतिर्महती, पतितः संग्रामसमयः, तत् कथं नाहूयते रणजम्बूकः सेनापतिः?

(प्रविश्य रणजम्बुकः परिक्रम्य सगर्वम्) - देअ! सुणीअदु अम्हाणं

बीरत्तणम् । (देव! श्रूयताम् अस्माकं वीरत्वम् ।)

राजा – कथय ।

रण – देअ! अज्ज मएरत्तपुष्परसं पिअंती अबलोइदा (देव! अद्य मया रक्तपुष्परसं पिबन्ती अवलोकिता ।)

राजा – ततः ।

रण – तदो सत्तरं अगं तणुतं णिबेसिअ खत्तिअचउट्टएण समं अस्तं धारिअ थुलचम्मरज्जुगृहिं आअट्टिदा । (ततः सत्वरम् अङ्गे तनुत्रं निवेश्य क्षत्रियचतुष्टयेन समम् अस्त्रं धृत्वा स्थूलचर्मरज्जुभिः आकृष्टा ।)

राजा – (सहर्षम्) । ततः?

रण – तदो तीक्खखग्गप्पहारेण चम्मकोमत्तणं णीदा (ततः तीक्ष्णखङ्गप्रहारेण चर्मकोषत्वं नीता ।)

राजा – तत्र कः सन्देहः ? नागायुतबलोऽसि ।

मन्त्री – भोः सोनापते? पतितः सङ्ग्रामसमयः, तव साहसः कीदृशः ।

रण – (प्रस्फुटं संस्कृतमाश्रित्य) –

सद्यो दत्तमलक्तकं पदयुगे दृष्ट्वाऽङ्गनाया रतौ
रक्तभ्रान्तिवशाद्भयेन नितरां ग्लानेन्द्रियो मेदिनीम् ।
पश्यन् दर्शनिशतमिस्त्रनिकरच्छन्नामिवाशां तथा
मूर्छेयं भुवि का कथा समरतो रक्तस्य सक्तद्विषाम् ? ।।44।।

मृगा – (उच्चैर्हसति) ।

रण – (सक्रोधम्) । आः!! पामरि गणिए! मं उअहससि!! ता कुण मए समं समलं । (आः!! पामरि गणिके! माम् उपहससि!! तत् कुरु मया समं समरम् ।) (इति रोषं नाटयति) ।

(प्रविश्य प्रतीहारः संस्कृतमाश्रित्य) - देव! महायात्रिको नाम सांवत्सरिको द्वारि वर्त्तते ।

राजा –प्रवेशय ।
प्रती – (तथा कृत्वा निष्क्रान्तः) ।
(प्रविश्य महायान्त्रिकः पञ्चिजकां प्रसार्थ्यं दक्षिणाभिमुखः पठति)-
भवे भवतु भास्करः सुरगुरुस्तथा रन्ध्रगः,
खरांशुतनयोऽष्टमः सपदि मेदिनीनन्दनः ।
दिनेशगृहसङ्गतः स खलु सैंहिकेयो बली
फलं किमपरैः पुनः शशिकवीन्दुजातैर्ग्रहैः ? ।।45।।
मन्त्री – श्रुतः शुभाशीर्वादः, सम्प्रति संग्रामार्थी देवः, तत् क्रियतां महायात्रायाः क्षणः ।
महा – पूर्णिमासंयुक्तशनैश्चरवासरे श्रवणानक्षत्रे वृश्चिकलग्ने प्रातः समये देवस्य महायात्रा भविष्यति ।
कल – ता एत्थ मरणं जाअदि (तदत्र मरणं जायते ।)
महा – प्रजानामापदं नीत्या यातु नाम ।
विश्व – (पूर्वां पश्चिमां दिशञ्चावलोक्य) ।
भानुबिम्बमिदमस्तगामि च प्रोद्यतं कुमुदबन्धुमण्डलम् ।
दृश्यते रतिपतेः प्रवासिनां क्रोधरक्तमिव लोचनद्वयम् ।।46।।
(नायिकामवलोक्य सकामम्) । वत्स कलहांकुर! प्रवृत्तः सन्ध्यासमयः, तदस्याः कर्णे स्वैरं भण यथा त्वया सार्द्धं निभृतमस्माकं सन्ध्या
निर्वहति ।
कल – (आकर्ण्यात्मगतं संस्कृतमाश्रित्य) । दुष्टोऽयम् उपाध्यायः तरुणीं रन्तुकामः ।
अपि च –
किं मे सद्गुरुसेवनैः प्रतिदिनं? किं व्योमधामार्चनैः?
किं स्यादध्ययनेन वा? सुरपुरप्राप्त्याऽथवा किं फलम्?
एतस्याः कुचकुम्भनिर्भरपरीरम्भप्रभावोद्भव-
स्वेदाम्भोभिरनङ्गवह्निरधुना निर्वापितो नो यदि ।।47।।
भवतु, तत् अलं विलम्बेन, कथमेषा निर्भरमालिङ्ग्य न चुम्ब्यते? (उपसृत्य प्रकाशम्), मिअंकलेहे! किंपि जप्पिदुमिच्छेमि (मृगाङ्कलेखे । किमपि जल्पितुमिच्छामि ।)
मृगा – जइ जुत्तं, ता कधं ण भणासि ? (यदि युक्तं, तत् कथं न भणसि?)
कल – (संस्कृतमाश्रित्य) –
तारुण्यं दिवसानि पञ्च दश वा पीनस्तनोत्तम्भनं
नो जातं पुनरित्याहो! विधुमुखि! प्राणास्तु न स्थायिनः ।
ज्ञात्वैवं समुपेक्ष्यतेऽभ्युपगतो यद्वामदृष्ट्या युवा
न स्थैर्य्यं कुचयोर्हृदि स्थिरतरं जागर्त्ति शल्यं हि तत् ? ।।48।।
मृगा – (किञ्चित् स्मयति) ।
कल - मिअंकलेहे! किंपि रहस्सं जप्पेमि, सुणादु भोदी । (मृगाङ्कलेखे! किमपि रहस्यं जल्पासि, श्रृणोतु भवती ।) (इति श्रुतिमूले मिलित्वा निर्भरमालिङ्ग्य उच्चैश्चुचुम्ब । संस्कृतमाश्रित्य ।)
स्वादितं सुदशनच्छदसीधु नामरैर्विधुरबुद्धिभिरस्याः ।
यद्विधुन्तुदमुखादवशिष्टः पीयते प्रमुदितैर्हारिणाङ्कः ।।49।।
विश्व - (सक्रोधम्) । अरे पामर बटो!मत्काङ्क्षितां नायिकामालिङ्गसि चुम्बसि च, अतः प्रायश्चित्ती त्वम् ।
कल – अहं ण, तुमं, जदो सिस्सालिगिदां णाइआं मक्कांखिदां जप्पेसि । (अहं न, त्वं, यतः शिष्यालिङ्गितां नायिकां मत्काङ्क्षितां जल्पसि ।)
विश्व – यस्याङ्गस्य योगात् गजो हस्तीत्युच्यते तदभिधानमङ्गं तव छेद्यं भवति, येन गुरुवाञ्छिता नायिका स्पृष्टा ।
कल - अंगणाजहणरज्जणणामहेअं अंगं तुह बिच्छेज्जं भोदि, जेण सिस्सपरिचुंबिदां णाइआं स्वबांछिदां जप्पेसि । (अङ्गनाजघनरञ्जननामधेयम् अङ्गं तव विच्छेद्यं भवति, येन शिष्यपरिचुम्बितां नायिकां स्ववाञ्छितां जल्पसि ।)
विश्व – अधरो यस्याच्छादनं तस्योत्पाटनं युक्तं, येन अस्या अधरः

पीडितः ।

कल - लिगिप्पेरणेति धातुणोरच्-पच्चएण जं रूअं सिज्झं भोदि तुह तस्स उप्पाटणं जोग्गं, जेण सिस्सचुंबिदां णाइआं पेच्छसि! ('लिगि प्रेरणे' इति धातोरच्-प्रत्ययेन यद्रूपं सिद्धं भतवि, तव तस्य उत्पाटनं योग्यः, येन शिष्यचुम्बितां नायिकां प्रेक्ष्यसि ।) (इति अन्योऽन्यं कलहं कुर्वाणो नृत्यतः । सर्वे हसन्ति ।)

(नेपथ्ये वैतालिकः)- शुभसन्ध्यासमयोऽस्तु दिवसस्य ।

गाढं प्रौढाङ्गनाभिः सुरतरतमनःसम्मदोत्सारिताक्षं
मुग्धाभिस्त्रस्तनेत्रं रतिसमरभयं चिन्तयन्तीभिरेवम् ।
पन्थानामङ्गनाभिः ससलिलनयनं शून्यचित्ताभिरुच्चैः
कष्टं दृष्टोऽस्तशैलं भृशमसजदयं मण्डलश्चण्डरश्मेः ।।50।।

अपि च –

गतवति दिननाथे पश्चिमक्ष्माधरान्तं
शिशिरकरमयूखैर्निर्भरं दह्यमाना ।
परिहृतमिलितालिः पान्थकान्तेव दीना
सपदि कमलिनीयं हास्यहीना बभूव ।।51।।

अपि च –

द्वितीयो वन्दी –

क्वैतत् मार्त्तण्डबिम्बं? सरसि सरसिजश्रेणिहास्यं क्व यातं?
क्वैते याता रथाङ्गाः? सपदि गतह्रियः क्व प्रविष्टा मरालाः?
सन्ध्यारागारुणाङ्गः कुपित इव पतिः प्रोद्यतोऽयं हिमांशु-
र्मन्ये हर्षादितीयं हसति कुमुदिनी जाग्रतीवालिनादैः ।।52।।

अपि च –

स्वर्धामामृतपानचारुचषकं किं? कामदेवाङ्गना-
क्रीडाकन्दुक एष किं? सुरनदीहिण्डीरपिण्डः किमु ? ।
किं छत्रं स्मरभूपतेः ? किमु यशःपुञ्जं पुरस्तादिदं
चेतःसंशयकारकं समुदितं शीतद्युतेर्मण्डलम् ।।53।।

मन्त्री - प्रवृत्तः सन्ध्याकालः तत् कथं नित्यक्रियायै न गम्यते ?

राजा - किं तेन ? चौरचक्रभयात् चिन्ताकुलोऽस्मि । भवतु, तथाऽपि यास्यामि, क्षणं विरम, दृश्यतामनयोर्गुरुशिष्ययोर्विरोधः ।

विश्व - (दण्डहस्तः सामर्षं धावति ।)

कल - (उच्चैः शीत्कृत्य सर्वाङ्गं पुलकयति ।)

(ततोऽन्योऽन्यं नायिकाऽञ्चलं गृहीत्वा "मम इयम्" इति उच्चार्य्य कलहायमानौ नृत्यतः ।)

बन्धु – (पुरः परिक्रम्य) । अज्ज भअबं! चिट्ठदु अज्ज कलहो, समीअबट्टिणी रअणी बट्टदि, पत्तुसहोमात्थं मअणांधमिस्सो आगमिस्सदि, सो क्खु जं आदिसदि तं कादब्बं । (आर्य! भगवन्! तिष्ठतु अद्य कलहः । समीपवर्त्तिनी रजनी वर्त्तते, प्रत्यूषहोमार्थं मदनान्धमिश्रः आगमिष्यति, स खलु यदादिशति तत् कर्त्तव्यम् ।)

उभौ – तथा अस्तु ।

(इति निष्क्रान्ताः सर्वे) ।

इति हास्यार्णवे प्रहसने सभानिर्णयो नाम प्रथमोऽङ्कः ।

द्वितीयोऽङ्कः

(ततः प्रातः प्रविशति विश्वभण्डः शिष्यश्च)

विश्व – (प्राचीमवलोक्य) अहो! दिगङ्गनाशिरःसिन्दूरशोभेव दिनकरकिरणावली दृश्यते । (परिक्रम्य पुरो वापीमवलोक्य च ।)

अन्यत्र वञ्चितनिशं परिलोहिताङ्ग
मन्याङ्गनागतमिवागतमुष्णरश्मिम् ।
प्रातर्निरीक्ष्य कुपितेव हि पद्मिनीयम्
उत्फुल्लहल्लकसुलोहितलोचनाऽभूत् ।।1।।

अपि च –

नारीणां मृगनाभिकुङ्कुमरसप्रक्षालनश्यामलान्
सम्भोगश्रमशीकरान् परिहरन्नाकम्पयन् कुन्तलान् ।
पुष्पामोदमनोरमान् विगलितानम्भोजगन्धं वहन्
प्रातस्त्यः पवनो वहत्ययमतिस्वान्तप्रमोदप्रदः ।।2।।

(उभौ परिक्रम्य बन्धुरायाः प्राङ्गणमुपसृत्य प्रविष्टौ युगपत्) । क्व सा बन्धुरा नायिका च ?

(ततः प्रविशति बन्धुरा नायिका च ।)

विश्व – (मृगाङ्कलेखामवलोक्य ।) –

अस्याः शरच्छशधरप्रतिमाननायाः
किञ्चित्कटाक्षमिलिता यदि नैव दृष्टिः ।
तत् केन लक्ष्यत इदं किल कर्णलग्न-
मिन्दीवरं मृदुलमञ्जनपत्त्ररम्यम् ? ।।3।।

अपि च

निद्रया परिघूर्णनशीला बलदूर्ध्वतारका लोलाः ।
अस्या नयननिपाताः दुःसहनीया हरस्यापि ।।4।।

कल - बंधुरे! दणिंपि णाआदो मअणांधमिस्सो? (बन्धुरे! इदानीमपि नायातो मदनान्धमिश्रः?)

(नेपथ्ये)

वेश्याऽङ्गरागरसलोहितयज्ञसूत्रः
शक्राशनाशनविलोहिततारनेत्रः ।
आभालपूर्णतिलको हृतधर्मकृच्छ्रः
संसर्पति स्वयमयं मदनान्धमिश्रः ।।5।।

(ततः प्रविशति शिष्येण कुलालनामधेयेन अनुगम्यमानो मदनान्धमिश्रः ।)

(समन्तादवलोक्य) अहो! भ्रमद्भ्रमरावलीवलयितरसालबकुलः कोकिलकलध्वनिजनितविषादविरहिणीजनपीवरनिःश्वासानिलः कुसुमकालो वर्त्तते ।

अपि च –

कावेरीनीरखेलद्युवतिहतिभवच्छीकरासङ्गशीतः
श्रीखण्डामादवाही प्रमुदितमदनप्राणविश्रामधामा ।
किञ्चिद्व्याधूतचूतद्रुममुकुलकुलः पुष्पवत्या लताया
भीतः स्पर्शादिवायं प्रसरति पवनो दक्षिणो मन्दमन्दम् ।।6।।

(आत्मगतम्) । कथं मया अस्मिन् मधौ गणिकां विना जीवनीयम्? (प्रकाशम्) वत्स कुलाल! पश्य मध्याह्नः संवृत्तः । -

मार्त्तण्डश्चण्डतापैः प्रतपति वसुधां पत्त्रिणः कुञ्जसंस्थाः
प्रोत्फुल्लाम्भोजराजीतलशरणगता निश्चला राजहंसाः ।
पान्थाः श्रान्ताश्च कान्ताचिरविरहशिखिज्वालया प्लुष्टचिताः
स्थाणुच्छायासु लीनाः क्षितिलिखनपराः सन्ततं निःश्वसन्ति ।।7।।

वत्स – कस्याश्रमे भोजनसिद्धिः अस्तु ?

कुला - अज्ज! अत्थि दाव एत्थज्जेब णअरे बंधुरा णाम कुट्टिणी, सा क्खु अदिधीणं परिचज्जं करेदित्ति सुणीअदि, ता अज्ज तत्त ज्जेब भोअ

णसिज्झि । (आर्य अस्ति तावद् अत्रैव नगरे बन्धुरा नाम कुट्टिनी, सा खलु अतिथीनां परिचार्यां करोति इति श्रूयते, तदद्य तत्रैव भोजनसिद्धिः ।)

मद – कुलीना सा ?

कुला - एत्थ को सण्णेहो? चंडालोबि अस्स घरे पाणीअं ण पीअदि । (अत्र कः सन्देहः? चण्डालोऽपि अस्याः गृहे पानीयं न पिबति ।)

मद - (सोत्साहम्) । वत्स! तदुपसर्पावः । (इत्यभौ परिक्रम्य बन्धुरायाः प्राङ्गणमुपसृत्य उपविष्टौ) ।

बन्धुरा - अज्ज! एदं भद्दासणं उअबिसदु मिस्सो । (आर्य! इदं भद्रासनम् उपविशतु मिश्रः) ।

मद – (नाट्येन उपविश्य सर्वानवलोक्य च आत्मागतम् ।) अहो! आश्चर्यं पुरतो नायिकारत्नम् ?

सायं चन्द्रकलायुतोदयगिरिस्पर्द्धां दधानौ स्तनौ
शैलोत्तुङ्गतरौ नखाङ्करुचिरौ शोणाम्बराभ्यन्तरे ।
अस्याः कं न विलोकनोत्कमकरोत् तीक्ष्णः कटाक्षः क्षणं
भृङ्गाकृष्टगरिष्ठकेतकदलभ्रान्तिं वहन्नप्ययम् ? ।।8।।

अपि च –

उत्तुङ्गस्तनशैलदुस्तरमुरो निम्नाऽति नाभिस्थली
भीमं देहवनं स्फुरद्भुजलतं लोमालिजालाकुलम् ।
व्याधः पञ्चशरःकिरत्यतितरांस्तीक्ष्णान् कटाक्षाशुगान्
तन्मे ब्रूहि मनःकुरुङ्ग! शरणं कं साम्प्रतं यास्यसि ? ।।9।।

(पुनः सविमर्षम्) । कथमेतौ कितवौ वञ्चनीयौ? भवतु तावदात्मनो वैष्णवत्वं प्रकटीकृत्य वञ्चयामि । (प्रकाशम्) –

जिह्वे!ऽनिशं हरिरिति स्मर लोचन! त्वं
व्याप्तं विलोकय जगद्धरिणा समस्तम् ।
आकर्णय श्रवण! कीर्तिकथा मुरारे-
र्नारायणं शरणमाश्रय चित्त! नूनम् ।।10।।

(पुनरात्मगतम्) । आः !! जातं हरिस्मरणेन महापातकं, किं करिष्यामि प्रायश्चित्तमात्मनः?

विश्व – (आकर्ण्यात्मगतम्) । धूर्तोऽयं मिश्रः कैतवं प्रकटयति । भवतु, अहमपि किञ्चित् प्रकटयामि । (प्रकाशम्) –

त्रैलोक्यमौलिमुकुटाञ्चितनीलरत्नं
पद्मालयावदनतामरसद्विरेफम् ।
दैत्याङ्गनानयनतोयनिपातधूमं
कृष्णं सदैव मनसा परिचिन्तयामि ।।11।।

मद – (सरोषम्) । वत्स! कुलाल! पठ वैष्णवधर्मम् ।

कुला - अज्ज! जं आणबेदि । (आर्य! यदाज्ञापयति।) (इति संस्कृतमाश्रित्य पठति ।) –

आयुः क्षीणमिदं परं कलियुगे दैवात्ततः पामरैः
लोकैरप्युपवासकष्टविधिना व्यर्थं वपुः क्षीयते ।
ज्ञात्वैवं सुधियो विहाय विविधक्लेशव्रतं निष्फलं
नानाभोगविलासिनीरसयुतं धर्मं भजन्ते द्रुतम् ।।12।।

विश्व - (सक्रोधम्) । वत्स कलहांकुर! पठवैष्णवधर्मम् ।

कल - (संस्कृतमाश्रित्य पठति)-

कृत्वा लोकभयान्नृणां जडधियां कष्टोपवासं निशा-
काले प्राणविनाशसंशयकरीं सोढ्वाऽपि मर्मव्यथाम् ।
प्रातश्चेद्यदि जीवितं स्थितमिह प्राप्तिस्तथाऽप्यन्धसः
साक्षाज्जीवनसंशयः प्रथमतो मुक्तिः परीक्षा क्व सा? ।।13।।

अपि च –

क्लेशोपवासविधिना सुकृतं वदन्ति
ये तन्मुखं सपदि पूरय भस्मपुञ्जैः ।
एकः प्रसीदति यदा जगदीशशम्भुः
मुक्तिस्तदा पिशितमीनसुराऽङ्गनाभिः ।।14।।

मद – (आकर्ण्यात्मगतम्) । धूर्तोऽयम् उपाध्यायो वञ्चयितुम् अशक्यः, जीर्णमार्जारं काञ्जिकया प्रतारयितुं न शक्यते । भवतु, विनयेन वञ्चयामि । (प्रकाशम्) । भगवन्!अयमहमभिवादये ।

विश्व - (उच्चैः) । आयुष्मान् भव सौम्य! किञ्च अयुक्तमेतत् भवादृशां यद्वाराङ्गनाऽग्रतो मयि प्रथममभिवादनम् ।

मद- अहो! वेश्याभ्रमेण भवत्सु प्रणामः कृतः ।

विश्व - (विहस्य)! सत्यमेव मदनान्धोऽसौ, यतः पुंसि अपि वेश्याभ्रमः ।

मद – (उपसृत्य) । वाराङ्गने! त्वमहं प्रणमामि ।

बन्धु-पुत्ति! उट्ठिअ आसिसं कुण । (पुत्रि! उत्थाय आशिषं कुरु ।)

मृगा – (उत्थाय) । गौरी दे सुप्पसण्ण होदु । (गौरी ते सुप्रसन्ना भवतु ।)

(इति लज्जां नाटयति ।)

मद - अहो! आश्चर्यमस्याः-

पादाभ्यामतिविपुलो नितम्ब एषः
प्रोद्वोढुं कथमपि शक्यते मृगाक्ष्याः ।
एकाकी वहति कथं नु मध्यभागः
प्रोत्तुङ्गस्तनकरिकुम्भयुग्मभारम् ? ।।15।।

बन्धु - अज्ज !बिप्पअर !बिज्जबेमि अज्ज अम्हाणं गेहे कंदप्पहोमो बट्टदि, तं णिब्बाहअदु मिस्सो । (आर्य! विप्रवर! विज्ञापयामि, अद्य अस्माकं गृहे कन्दर्पहोमो वर्त्तते, तं निर्वाहयतु मिश्रः ।)

वेदी सज्जघनञ्च तत्परिसरे कुण्डं वराङ्गं फलं
नैवेद्याय कुचद्वयं मृगदृशः कामानलः प्रोज्ज्वलः ।
होताऽहं खलु शुक्रहव्यनिवहः शेफःस्रु वो वर्त्तते
नित्यं पञ्चशराध्वरं त्यजति कः सद्यः सुखं यत्फलम्? ।।16।।

(प्रकाशम्) । बन्धुरे!त्वमतिजीर्णा अकार्यकुशला च, तन्नियोजय स्वपुत्रीं यज्ञसामग्रीकरणाय ।

बन्धु - पुत्ति! तुमं बिप्पअरशासणं कुण । (पुत्रि! त्वं विप्रवरशासनं कुरु।)

(मुगाङ्कलेखा गृहं प्रविशति) ।

(उपसृत्य कलहांकुरः) । पढमं अम्हाणं गुरुसिस्साणं णाअं बिचारी मदु अज्जमिस्सो । (प्रथमम् अस्माकं गुरुशिष्याणां न्यायं विचारयतु

आर्यमिश्रः ।

मद - वत्स! क्षणं विरम, यावत् क्रतुकिया निर्वर्त्तते ।

(इति गृहं प्रविश्य निर्भरं सुरतं निर्वाह्य सहर्षम् ।)

आश्लेषपीडितकुचं श्रमघर्मितास्यं
दष्टाधरं ललितशीत्कृतमीलिताक्षम् ।
चाटूक्तिचारुललितभ्रुचलत्कटाक्षं
वेश्यारतं जनिशतार्जितपुण्यलभ्यम् ।।17।।

(परिक्रम्य बहिः गच्छति । नायिका च परिक्रामति ।)

विश्व – (नायिकामवलोक्य आत्मगतम्) ।

यन्नेत्रं गलिताञ्जनं सुललितं निर्मुक्तरागोऽधरो
धम्मिल्लः श्लथबन्धनः श्रमजलप्रक्षालितं चन्दनम् ।
निष्पन्दं जघनं भुजे शिथिलता वक्षःस्थलं कम्पते
तत् सत्यं सुरतं विधाय सुतरामेषा समागच्छति ।।18।।

कुला– (पुरः साट्टहासम्) । अज्ज! एक्केण णिब्बाहिदा कदुविक्कआ । (आर्य! एकेन निर्वाहिता क्रतुक्रिया ।)

मद - (दक्षिणाक्षिसङ्कोचं निवारयति) ।

कुला – किं णिआरणेण? अण्णस्स पुण्णेण किं अण्णो पूदोभोदि? (किं निवारणेन? अन्यस्य पुण्येन किम् अन्यः पूतो भवति?)

मद - वत्स! क्षणं विरम ।

विश्व – (सस्मितम्) । महामिश्र! ज्ञातेयं ते क्रतुक्रिया । भवतु, तथाऽपि विचार्यतामावयोर्न्यायः । (कर्णे स्वैरम्) । यथेयं मृगाङ्कलेखा मया परिणीता भवति तदनुष्ठेयम् ।

मद-आवाभ्यां परिणेतव्या एषा ।

विश्व - को दोषः ? पश्य ।

धर्मादिपञ्चपतिभिः खलु पाण्डुना च
युक्ता सती भवति भोजसुता च कुन्ती
धर्मात्मजादिभिरिहोपगता च कृष्णा
एका बहून् यदि भजेत् वद कोऽत्र दोषः ? ।।19।।

कुला – (आत्मगतम्)! आभ्यां धूर्ताभ्यां मिलितम् । भवतु, आहमपि कलहांकुरेण समं सख्यं करोमि । (इति परिक्रम्य कलहांकुरस्य कण्ठमालिङ्ग्य कर्णे स्वैरम्) । बअस्स! पेक्खस्स एदेहिं गुरुएहिं मिलिदं, एषा मिअंकलेहा एदेहिं ज्जेब परिणेदब्बा, ता कधं अम्हेहि एसा बंधुरा णो परिणीअदि ? (वयस्य! प्रेक्षस्व एताभ्यां मिलितम्, एषा मृगाङ्कलेखा एताभ्यामेव परिणेतव्या, तत् कथमावाभ्याम् एषा बन्धुरा न परिणीयते?)

कल - बअस्स! भद्दं ण भणिदं, जदो अम्हाणं बि बुढ्बा सुरदं ण बिस्सादं, इदं उण एक्कं पअमं दुक्खं एसा तिहुअणमोहिणी बुड्बेहिं परिणेदब्बा; ण हि मालइमाला बाणरहत्थगदा सोहइ, ण हि कत्थुरिआगुणग्गामं कुग्गामिणो जाणंति, ण हि गलिदजोब्बणाए बक्खत्थले मोत्तिअमाला सोहइ । (वयस्य! भद्रं न भणितं, यतः अस्माकपि वृद्धासुरत न विज्ञातम् । इदं पुनरेकं परमं दुःखम्, एषा त्रिभुवनमोहिनी वृद्धाभ्यां परिणेतव्या, न हि मालतीमाला वानरहस्तगता शोभते, न हि कस्तूरिकागुणग्रामं कुग्रामिणो जानन्ति, न हि गलितयौवनायाः वक्षःस्थले मौक्तिकमाला शोभते ।)

कुला - बअस्स! एदेहिं ज्जेब बुढ्बेहिं कत्तिदिणं जीबिदब्बं? एदाणं लोआंतरगमणे एसा अम्हेहिं परिणेदब्बा । (वयस्य! एताभ्यामेव वृद्धाभ्यां कतिदिनानि जीवितव्यम्! एतयोः लोकान्तरगमने एषा आवाभ्यां परिणेतव्या ।)

कल - सच्चं, तधाऽबि पढ़मं दुक्खं । (सत्यं, तथाऽपि प्रथमं दुःखम् ।)

कुला-एहिंपि पदिबासरं एदाणं भिक्खाटणसमए एसा गेहबट्टिणी हुबिस्सदि, बंधुरा तु तिमिराउललोअणा, तदो अम्हाणं मणोरहसिज्झि । (इदानीमपि प्रतिवासरम् एतयोः भिक्षाटनसमये एषा गृहवर्त्तिनी भविष्यति, बन्धुरा तु तिमिराकुललोचना, तदा अस्माकं मनोरथसिद्धिः) ।

कल – भोदु जं भणसि बअस्स! (भवतु यत् भणसि वयस्य !)

बन्धु – (विहस्य आत्मगतम्) । मिलिदा सठेहिं, ताणं परिचिदं भोदि । (मिलितं शठाभ्यां, तयोः परिचितं भवति।)

मद-भो महामहोपाध्याय! कीदृशो युवयोर्न्यायः ? क्रियतां प्रश्नः ?

विश्व –अस्मत्काङ्क्षितां मृगाङ्कलेखाम् अयं परिणेतुमिच्छति ।

मद – भो कलहांकुर! तव प्रत्युत्तरं कीदृशम् ?

कल – एसा मिअंकलेहा मुए आलिंगिदा परिचुंबिदा अ, तधाऽबिएष इमां परिणेदुमिच्छति । (एषा मृगाङ्कलेखा मया आलिङ्गिता परिचुम्बिता च, तथाऽपि एष इमां परिणेतुम् इच्छति ।)

मद – अलं शुष्कचर्वणेन, ज्ञातं न्यायतत्त्वम् । एषा प्रथमत उपाध्यायेन कल्पिता, एतेन कथमपि अंशैकेन अस्य भवति, व्यवस्थापकत्वात् समन्तादस्माकं भवति । (पुनः ससम्भ्रमम्) ।

भो भो वत्स! यथा त्वं द्वादशवर्षीयो वरस्तथा च बन्धुरा, उपपतिगणनालेखामिव लेखां शरीरतो दधती कन्या इयं तव योग्या वर्षशतात् किञ्चिदपि अधिका ।

(उपसृत्य कुलालः संस्कृतमाश्रित्य) । व्यवस्थापकशिष्यत्वात् ममापि एषा भवति ।

मद – भो वत्स! कलहांकुर! भवतु एवं भवता मच्छिष्येण समम् एषा परिणीयताम् ।

कल- जधा सासणं बिप्पअस्स । (यथा शासनं विप्रवरस्य) ।

बन्धु- (सहर्षम् अत्यागतं संस्कृतमाश्रित्य) । अहो! मयि प्रसन्नः प्रजापतिः, यतो वार्द्धक्येऽपि तरुणपतिद्वयलाभः!

विश्व– (कलहांकुरम् अवलोक्य सस्मितम् आत्मगतम्) –

निष्क्रामति शिशोः कायो येन रन्ध्रेण योषितः ।
किं करिष्यति तत्रायं बटुः शिश्नशलाकया ? ।।20।।

(पुनः प्रकाशम्) । प्रत्यासन्नो विवाहोत्सवः, तत् कथं न आहूयते दक्षिणराढीयो महानिन्दकाचार्यः?

(प्रविश्य महानिन्दकाचार्यः सर्वानवलोक्य सदम्भम्) –

ब्रह्माण्डे के द्विजाः सन्ति पाण्डित्येन कुलेन वा ।
ये स्पर्द्धितुं मया सार्धं किञ्चिदावर्जितोद्यमाः? ।।21।।

(पुनः सगर्वम्) । मया रचिताश्चत्वारो वेदाः ।

कल - अज्ज! बम्हमूहणिग्गदा बेआ, ता कधं भवदा बिअइदा?

(आर्य! ब्रह्ममुखनिर्गताः वेदाः तत्कथं भवता विरचिताः?)

महा- (सक्रोधम्) आः क्षुद्रबुद्धिं ब्रह्माणं गणयसि? श्रृणु, तत्कौलीन्यपरीक्षार्थम् स्वर्गगतेन मया –

पाद्यं विष्णुपदीजलेन चरणे दत्तं शिरोवर्तिना
तत्क्रोधेन करप्रहारनिकरैः सन्ताडितः शङ्करः ।
आयुष्मान् न कृतो भयात् प्रणमति ब्रह्मण्यवज्ञावशाद्
नो दृष्टस्त्रिदशप्रतिग्रहपरः पापास्पदो गीष्पतिः ।।22।।

मद – अलं वाग्विस्तरेण, निर्वाह्यताम् अस्माकं विवाहद्वयम् ।

महा – अहम् अप्रतिग्राही ।

कुला – गणिआप्पतिग्गहे को दोषः ? (गणिकाप्रतिग्रहे को दोषः?)

महा – भद्रमुक्तम् एतत् पूर्वं न ज्ञायते कुलीना इयं वेश्या । (सादरम्) भगवन्!कया सह कस्य विवाहः ?

विश्व-

आवां योग्यावुपाध्यायौ वरावस्या मृगीदृशः ।
शिष्यावेतावमुष्यास्तु तिमिराकुलचक्षुषः ।।23।।

महा – (विहस्य आत्मगतम्) अहो! आश्चर्य्यम्

(पुनः मृगाङ्कलेखामवलोक्य) आश्चर्य्यम् अस्याः ।

प्रविशति कटाक्षविशिखे तीक्ष्णतरे भेदके च हृदयानाम् ।
तथाऽपि लक्ष्यीभूय स्थातुमपेक्षा भवेन्न कस्यापि? ।।24।।

अपि च –

दुग्धसमुद्रसमुत्थितविषमिव परिदुःसहा हरस्यापि ।
अस्या दृशि विमलायां तरलतरतारकाऽतिभीमा ।।25।।

किञ्चास्या निर्भरपरिरम्भणं विना न मया इदानीं जीनीयम् ।

(प्रकाशम्) ।

एतस्याः स्तनपद्मकोरकयुगं यस्याननेन्दोः सित-
ज्योत्स्नाभिर्न भजत्यदो मृगदृशः शङ्के प्रकाशं पुनः ।
तस्मिँल्लोचनपङ्कजं विकसितं भ्रूभङ्गसंसेवितं
स्वान्ते संशयमातनोति सुतरामेतन्ममैवासकृत् ।।26।।

अपि च –

अहो! मूढास्ते ।

पानायाधरतोऽमृतं वसतयेऽप्यस्याः स्तनक्ष्माधरो-
ऽधस्तात्सज्जघनान्तकन्दरधरः सख्याय चक्षुर्मृगः ।
जप्यो मन्त्रवरो मनोहरकथा ध्यानाय वक्त्राम्बुजं
चेत्थं देहतपःस्थले सति कथं सन्तो वनान्तं गताः ? ।।27।।

भो भोः! विश्वभण्ड! लग्नकरणार्थं कथं न आहूयते महायात्रिकनामा मौहूर्त्तिकः?

(प्रविश्य महायात्रिकः पञ्जिकां प्रसार्य) । भो भोः पण्डित! किं गणनीयम्?

मद- क्रियतां वैवाहिककक्षणः ।

महायात्रिकः – (भूमौ कठिनीं पातयित्वा) ।

यत्र कुत्रापि लग्ने च वासरे यस्य कस्यचित् ।
यत्र कुत्रापि नक्षत्रे यद्वा तद्वा विधीयताम् ।।28।।

महानिन्दकः – (स्वगतम्) । योग्य एष दैवज्ञः (प्रकाशम्) भो भोः! सांवत्सरिक! कदाचिदनेन वैधव्यं जायते?

महायात्रिकः- किं पुरुषहीना धरणी यदेतयोर्वैधव्यं भविष्यति?

महानिन्दकः –भो भो विश्वभण्डादयः! बिल्वमाल्यधारिणो यथोद्दिष्टतल्पे अनुसरथ ।

महायात्रिकः – (सहासम्) । युक्तं पुरुषाणां वध्यमानानां भूषणम् ।

(सर्वे यथोद्दिष्टतल्पे करग्रहं विधाय उपविशन्ति । वृद्धा पतिद्वयमध्यगता, नायिका च तथा सविषादम् आत्मगतम्) ।

श्रीगौरीपादपद्माच्चणमतिविजने जक्किदं सब्बआलं
णिच्चं चित्तेण भक्तीद्दढतलमणिसं जक्किदा पुप्फबाणे ।
तस्माज्जेबं प्पसाओ णिहिलसुरकिदो जो गुरुप्पाणदंडो
पच्चासस्णो बिहाओ बिसमतररुजा जीण्णबिप्पेहिदोहिम् ।।29।।

(श्रीगौरीपादपद्मार्चनमतिविजने यत् कृतं सर्वकालं
नित्यं चित्तेन भक्तिर्दृढतरमनिशं यत्कृता पुष्पबाणे ।
तस्मादेवं प्रसादो निखिलसुरकृतो यद् गुरुप्राणदण्डः
प्रत्यासन्नो विवाहो विषमतररुजा जीर्णविप्रद्वयाभ्याम् ।।29।।)

महानिन्दकः - भुजङ्ग! समानीयतां मधुपर्कः ।

(उपसृत्य भुजङ्गः) - अज्ज! महुणा अहाबो, अत्थि दुद्धं णीरंपि । (आर्य! मधुनः अभावः, अस्ति दुग्धं नीरमपि ।)

महानिन्दकः – समानय ।

भुजङ्गः – (समानीय अर्पयति) ।

महानिन्दकः – (प्रत्येकं वराभिमुखम्) ।

ओं श्मशानानलदग्धोऽसि परित्यक्तोऽसि बान्धवैः ।
इदं नीरमिदं क्षीरं स्नात्वा पीत्वा सुखी भव ।।30।।

(पुनर्दूर्वाऽक्षतमादाय)

मरणं प्राणिनां नित्यं जीवनं स्वप्नवद् भुवि ।
भवद्भिरिति विज्ञाय कर्त्तव्या नात्र शोचना ।।31।।

(पुनरुत्थाय उच्चैः)–

पितृकाननमेदिन्यां महाशय्याऽनुशायिभिः ।
सुचिरं स्थीयतां नित्यं महानिद्राऽवलम्बिभिः ।।32।।

(इति सर्वेषां मौलिषु दूर्वाऽक्षतम् अर्पयति) ।

महायात्रिकः – तत् युक्तं वराणां श्मशाने चिताशयनम् ।

महानिन्दकः – (उपसृत्य) भोः कलहांकुर! दीयतां प्रथमतः शतवर्षकन्यादानदक्षिणा ।

कल – (शक्राशनलड्डुकमर्पयति)

महानिन्दकः – स्वस्ति । (इति गृहीत्वा सानन्दं शिरसि निधाय) । ओं गायत्र्यै नमः । (इति भूमौ किञ्चित् त्यक्त्वा पुनर्थक्षयित्वा सोत्साहम्) ।

जनयति सुरतेषु मुदं प्रथयति पीयूषवर्षिणीं वाणीम् ।
रचयति लोचनकुतुकं स जयति शक्राशनानन्दः ।।33।।

बन्धु-कुलीणअरो आचाज्जो । (कुलीनवरः आचार्यः) ।

महानिन्दकः – (पुनरुपसृत्य) । भो भो भगवन् मिश्रः! प्रदीयतां कन्यादानदक्षिणा ।

उभौ-प्रतिपाल्यतामब्दचतुष्टयम् ।

महानिन्दकः – तावदेषा बन्धकीभवतु । (इति मृगाङ्कलेखाया हस्तं धृत्वा तया सह सहर्षं नृत्यति) ।

महायात्रिकः – भो भो महानिन्दकाचार्य्य! किमिदानीं भवतामपेक्षितमस्ति?

महानिन्दकः - (सहर्षम्) ।
लब्धेयं युवतिर्जगज्जनदृशामानन्दभूमिर्भृशं
धूर्त्तानां निकरं प्रवञ्च्य सहसा प्राप्ताश्च हृत्प्रीतयः ।
सम्प्रत्युद्भटसम्बरारिसमरं नानारतास्त्राङ्कितं
गत्वा केलिगृहं विधातुमधिकं वाञ्छा वरीवृत्यते ।।34।।
इति हास्यार्णवनामप्रहसनं समाप्तम् ।

REFERENCES

Apte, V. S. (2000). *The Student's Sanskrit-English Dictionary*. Delhi: Motilal Banarsidass Publishers.

Bhattacharya, B. (1973) (tr). *Daṇḍaviveka of Vardhamāna Upādhyāya*. Calcutta: The Asiatic Society.

Bhaṭṭachārya, J. (1977). *Hāsyārṇava: The Ocean of Laughter* (trans. Munda, R. D, & Nelson, D.). Calcutta: Writers Workshop.

Brooks, D. R. (1990). *The Secret of the Three Cities: An Introduction to Hindu Śākta Tantrism*. Chicago: The University of Chicago Press.

Dimock Jr., E. C. (1989). *The Place of the Hidden Moon: Erotic Mysticism in the Vaiṣṇava-sahajiyā Cult of Bengal*. Chicago: The University of Chicago Press.

Danielou, A. (1994). *The Complete Kāma Sūtra*. Rochester: Inner Traditions India.

Davis Jr, D. R. (2004). 'Being Hindu or Being Human: A Reappraisal of the Puruṣārthas'. *International Journal of Hindu Studies*, 8(1–3), 1–27.

Davis Jr, D. R. (2010). *The Spirit of Hindu Law*. New Delhi: Cambridge University Press.

Davis Jr, D. R. (2014). 'Satire as Apology: The Puruṣārtthakkūttŭ of Kerala'. In Veluthat, K., and Davis Jr, D. R. (Eds), *Irreverent History: Essays for M.G.S. Narayanan*. Delhi: Primus Books.

Debroy, B. (2013) (tr). *The Mahābhārata*, Volume 8. Gurgaon: Penguin Books.

Flood, G. (1997). 'The Meaning and Context of the Puruṣārthas'. In J. Lipner (Ed.), *The Fruits of Our Desiring: An Enquiry into the Ethics of the Bhagvadgītā*. Bayeux: Calgary.

Hansen, K. (1992). *Grounds for Play: The Nauṭankī Theatre of North India*. New Delhi: Manohar.

Hardy, F. (1990). 'Hinduism'. In U. King (Ed.), *Turning Points in Religious Studies: Essays in Honour of Geoffrey Parrinder*. Edinburgh: T & T Clark.

Hāsyārṇava Prahasana of Sri Jagadēśvara Bhaṭṭāchārya (1987). Edited with the 'Prabha Hindi Commentary by Ishwar Prasad Chaturvedi. Varanasi: Chowkhamba Vidyabhawan.

Heifetz, H. (2017) (tr). *Kalidasa's Kumarasambhava: The Origin of the Young God*. Gurgaon: Penguin Books.

Hiltebeitel, A. (2011). *Dharma: Its Early History in Law, Religion, and Narrative*. New York: Oxford University Press.

Lingat, R. (1993). *The Classical Law of India.* New Delhi: Munshiram Manoharlal Publishers Pvt. Ltd.
Malamoud, C. (1988). 'On the Rhetoric and Semantics of Puruṣārtha'. In T. N. Madan (Ed.). *Way of Life: King, Householder, Renouncer: Essays in Honour of Louis Dumont.* Delhi: Motilal Banarsidass Publishers.
McClish, M. (2018). 'King: Rājadharma'. In P. Olivelle and D. R. Davis Jr (Eds), *Hindu Law: A New History of Dharmaśāstra.* New Delhi: Oxford University Press.
McClish, M. (2018). 'Legal Procedure: Vyavahāra'. In P. Olivelle and D. R. Davis Jr (Eds), *Hindu Law: A New History of Dharmaśāstra.* New Delhi: Oxford University Press.
McClish, M. (2018). 'Punishment: Daṇḍa'. In P. Olivelle and D. R. Davis Jr (Eds), *Hindu Law: A New History of Dharmaśāstra.* New Delhi: Oxford University Press.
Miller, B. S. (Ed.) (tr) (1984). *Gītagovinda of Jayadeva: Love Song of the Dark Lord.* Delhi: Motilal Banarsidass Publishers.
Monier-Williams, M. (1999). *A Sanskrit-English Dictionary.* Delhi: Motilal Banarsidass Publishers.
Olith, A. B. (1924). *The Sanskrit Drama in Its Origin, Development, Theory and Practice.* London: Oxford University Press.
Olivelle, P. (1998). 'Brihadaranyaka Upanishad'. In *Upaniṣads*, A New Translation by Patrick Olivelle. Oxford: Oxford University Press.
Olivelle, P. (Ed.). (1999). *The Dharmasutras: The Law Codes of Ancient India.* Oxford: Oxford University Press.
Olivelle, P. (2009). *The Law Codes of Manu*, A New Translation by Patrick Olivelle. Oxford and New York: Oxford University Press.
Olivelle, P. (2013). *King, Governance and Law in Ancient India: Kauṭilya's Arthaśāstra*, A New Annotated Translation by Patrick Olivelle. New Delhi: Oxford University Press.
Olivelle, P. (2016). *A Dharma Reader: Classical Indian Law.* (trans Olivelle, P.). Ranikhet: Permanent Black in association with Ashoka University.
Rocher, L. (2012). *Studies in Hindu Law and Dharmashastra.* Donald R. Davis, Jr. (Ed.). London: Anthem Press.
Śatapatha Brāhmaṇa (2013). Weber, A. (Ed). Varanasi: Chowkhamba Sanskrit Series.
Shulman, D. D. (1984). 'The Enemy Within: Idealism and Dissent in South Indian Hinduism'. In S. N. Eisenstadt, R. Kahane and D. D. Shulman (Eds), *Orthodoxy, Heterodoxy, and Dissent in India.* Berlin: Mouton Publishers.
Shulman, D. D. (1985). *The King and the Clown in South Indian Myth and Poetry.* Princeton, NJ: Princeton University Press.
Siegel, L. (1987). *Laughing Matters: Comic Tradition in India.* Chicago: University of Chicago Press.
Smith, B. K. (1994). *Classifying the Universe: The Ancient Indian Varṇa System and the Origins of Caste.* New York: Oxford University Press.
Squarcini, F. (2011). 'Pāṣaṇḍin, vaitaṇḍika, vedanindaka and nāstika. On Criticism, Dissenters and Polemics and the South Asian Struggle for the Semiotic Primacy of Veridiction'. *Orientalia Suecana* LX, pp.101–115.
The Śiva-Purāṇa, Part II. (2008). (Translated by a board of scholars). Delhi: Motilal Banarsidass Publishers.
Veluthat, Kesavan (2013). *Of Ubiquitous Heroines and Elusive Heroes: The Cultural Milieu of Medieval Maṇipravāḷa Kāvyas from Kerala.* New Delhi: ICHR.
Zvelebil, K. V. (1973). *The Poets of the Powers: Freedom, Magic, and Renewal.* California: Integral Publishing.